Praise for **HOW DO I UN-REMEMBER THIS?**

"Danny Pellegrino is a delight, and so are his stories!"

—*New York Times* bestselling author Andy Cohen

"Danny Pellegrino is a national treasure. Reading his book is like spending time with the BFF of your dreams. His knowledge of pop culture is unrivaled, and his humor is unmatched. I'm both happy for him and seething with jealousy."

—Casey Wilson, *New York Times* bestselling author of *The Wreckage of My Presence*

"It is impossible not to fall in love with Danny in this heartfelt and deeply funny book. I laughed so hard I scared my kids. Randomly open to any page and you'll find a gem."

—Kate Baer, #1 *New York Times* bestselling author of *What Kind of Woman*

"I first met and loved Danny through his podcast, but I have come to understand him on a deeper level through the pages of his vulnerable, hilarious, and captivating book. Each essay is an adventure and brings a warm sense of nostalgia to the audience with witty and timeless pop cultural references. So, to use a pop culture reference from the '90s, 'I don't care who you are, where you're from, what you did,' you will see some version of yourself in his words, journey, and truth. Not only will you laugh—and possibly cry—but you will also end up learning more about Danny and, inevitably, yourself."

—Rachel Lindsay, media personality and author of *Miss Me with That*

"This makes me nervous. I'm not sure I should read it."

—Linda Pellegrino (Danny's mom)

HOW DO I UN-REMEMBER THIS?

UNFORTUNATELY TRUE STORIES

DANNY PELLEGRINO

sourcebooks

Published by Sourcebooks
P.O. Box 4410, Naperville, Illinois 60567-4410
(630) 961-3900
sourcebooks.com

Library of Congress Cataloging-in-Publication Data

Names: Pellegrino, Danny, author.
Title: How do I un-remember this? : unfortunately true stories / Danny
   Pellegrino.
Description: Naperville : Sourcebooks, 2022.
Identifiers: LCCN 2021052687 (print) | LCCN 2021052688 (ebook)
Subjects: LCSH: Pellegrino, Danny. | Comedians--United States--Biography. |
   Podcasters--United States--Biography. | Gays--United States--Biography.
Classification: LCC PN2287.P365 A3 2022 (print) | LCC PN2287.P365 (ebook)
   | DDC 791.46092 [B]--dc23/eng/20211116
LC record available at https://lccn.loc.gov/2021052687
LC ebook record available at https://lccn.loc.gov/2021052688

Printed and bound in the United States of America.
LSC 10 9 8 7 6 5 4 3 2 1

"Everyone has a story."

—KATHIE LEE GIFFORD

Contents

Introduction

Hi! Thank you so much for giving *How Do I Un-Remember This?* a read! Recently, I had some old family movies transferred to digital copies. When I showed them to my parents, my mother asked me five times if I had someone CGI the couches in the videos featuring our first house, because she doesn't remember owning them. Transferring vintage VHS tapes to a digital file is already expensive enough, so I'm not sure why she thinks I have the budget to hire Lucasfilm to update the sofas we owned in 1996, but the point is that everyone remembers the past a little bit differently. In this book, I'll tell some of the stories that shaped me the way I recall them, and hopefully you'll find a laugh or two. I purposefully changed some of the names, locations, and other details so no one gets too mad at me, because as a certified Libra, people being mad at me is at the top of the list of things I hate the most—alongside rats, unprovoked caricature artists, and that Claymation holiday special where Rudolph's nose sounds like a combination of a Furby with weak batteries and Fran Drescher stubbing her toe.

I've kept journals off and on throughout my life, so I've written about a lot of these things before, but just for my own eyes. I still have most of them, but there was one time I left one of my notebooks on a Chicago train, so somewhere, a Midwest vagabond is reading about the lingering trauma of the accidental erection I got in the fifth grade when my teacher let us watch *Ed*, the Matt LeBlanc movie where he plays baseball with a monkey. The first time I wrote in a diary was when I was a preteen, but I got consistent around twenty-one. That's when my mental health struggles ramped up, I started inching out of the closet, and I began chasing my Hollywood dreams of becoming a writer/performer. I look back on that first adult journal and recognize now that it was truly an unhinged piece of work. On one page, you can see tear-soaked ink and a detailed essay about coming out to my parents, and the next page is filled with movie ideas, half jokes, and comedy routines that I was trying to work out as a young comedian. Many of those bits don't make any sense, just disparate nouns posing as ideas. I pulled out that diary to prep for this book, and there's an entire page that just says, "Foghorn Leghorn is a less dramatic Tennessee Williams," and another where I simply wrote, "Nikki Blonsky as Catwoman." I wasn't even on drugs, I do declare; I had just seen *Hairspray*.

I have always been a mix of silliness and drama, with pop culture holding me together, and that love of entertainment runs deep. I've never had a second glass of wine that didn't end with me on Allison Janney's IMDB page. My mother is a similar blend, although not as deep of a movie/TV lover, but she did teach me all about the divas: the queens, icons, and legends of music. Whitney Houston, Céline Dion, Mariah Carey, Cher, Toni Braxton, and Gloria Estefan were all in heavy rotation throughout my childhood. Mom also has the best sense of humor and an infectious laugh that is my favorite thing of all time. There is nothing better than when she has the church giggles, laughing at all the ridiculousness around her. Otherwise, she's all heart with some drama mixed in. I like to think I'm more emotionally stable than she is, but that time I listened to Shania Twain's "It Only Hurts When I'm Breathing" on repeat *six months after* a breakup would beg to differ. My dad is a different concoction. He's a hard shell with a soft center—a short temper that often masks his other sides. He, too, has a great sense of humor, but he prefers laughing at pratfalls and fart jokes rather than observing the absurdity around him. There's a scene in *Dumb and Dumber* where the Jeff Daniels character is taking a very foul bathroom break on a date, and my dad still watches it with an uncontrollable, guttural chuckle and tears in his eyes, regardless of how many times he's seen it. Fart jokes may be the lowest common denominator of comedy, but maybe we should all accept the laughs wherever we can get them.

All that's to say: Welcome! Throughout these pages you'll get to know my parents and some of the other people closest to me, like my brothers, friends, and grandma, who have shaped me along the way. I hope you'll get to know me better too, but most importantly, I hope some of these stories will remind you of your own life and some of the funny memories you've made along the way.

A few years back, I started a podcast called *Everything Iconic with Danny Pellegrino*, where I recap reality TV and pop culture and interview celebrities about their work. Early on, I started sprinkling in these life stories. I'd be talking about *The Real Housewives* and then I'd say, "Let's take a little detour," as I segued into a tale about my child-hood. Pretty soon, those anecdotes became the things most people asked me about on social media or when I'd see them out and about. I started to contemplate that word, *detour*, and everything it entails. The idea of thinking we're on one path and then suddenly being forced to take another is such a heavy, relatable concept. No matter how old you are or what your profession is, I think we all have moments in our lives when we look around and realize things look different than what we had planned. There's an old Lee Ann Womack song called "I Hope You Dance," which is midtempo and not quite a romantic ballad suitable for slow dancing but also not really a party anthem that you would hear at a club. It's almost impossible to dance to, yet I believe the message of the song is you should try to do it anyway. Attempt the impossible. Those new roads might not be easy or kind, but they're part of the life ride.

So, without further ado, it's time to embrace the silly and the sad and take a few detours. And always remember, I hope *you* dance.

Emotionally Streaking

"I want what every man wants. Breakfast."

COYOTE UGLY (2000)

There's an art to the adult slumber party, and no, I'm not talking about the sexual kind (although those also require a unique set of talents). I'm referring to having some friends over for a night of being basic: frozen margaritas, *Coyote Ugly*, inhaling every last crumb of a charcuterie plate, and gossiping until the sun comes up. The gossip part is where my skills really shine. I've been doing that ever since I was a closeted kid in Ohio, embracing the metaphorical tea with whoever was willing to spill it at my local pajama party. It wasn't always easy to find other kids my age who wanted to chat about living, laughing, and loving in the '90s, but fortunately there were moms for that, and there's no one better than a mom.

When I was ten and under, slumber parties meant a movie, some pizza, me wrapped in a *Teenage Mutant Ninja Turtles* sleeping bag by 9:00 p.m., and then waking up early to talk to my friend's mother before any of the other kids got up. Breakfast with the woman of the household was my favorite part of the experience. This all usually happened at my best friend Bobby's house, an only child who always had the best snacks. His mom, Deborah, would sit me down in the nook and vent to me about her husband, Rick, and I loved the adultness of it. She didn't look at me like I was a kid; she treated me like the therapist she should've paid good money for. By the time we sat together, Deb often looked defeated, like she needed five more minutes of sleep and two fewer Valiums to properly get ready for her day, but I was able to perk her up just by listening. I always assumed a.m.'s were most difficult for her since she was coming from spending hours alone in a bed with her nightmare husband. Deb would pour me a glass of OJ and tell me about Rick working late and not caring about her thriving herb garden, while I would wonder how anyone could not be enamored by this amazing woman. She would make her coffee, "strong like an ox," as I sat beside her with a frosted strawberry Pop-Tart, ready to listen to her marital problems. I didn't have all the answers, but I would remind her that she was "strong like an ox," just like her coffee. And then, like clockwork, I would spot a lone tear cascading down her cheek before Rick interrupted our chat with some outdated demand, like that she needs to make him breakfast.

"Make your own fucking breakfast, Rick," I wanted to say. If I could turn back in time, I would take a wrecking ball to the patriarchy of that household. But alas, there is no time-traveling DeLorean for me to hop into (yet).

As adolescence hit, the sleepovers started to get weirder and weirder. The tween years are a strange time for kids, with everyone growing up at different rates and having various degrees of body odor, hair, and hormones. When I was twelve, I still wanted to do the little kid things like play with *Mighty Morphin Power Rangers* action figures, while the other kids wanted to call up girls from our class and playfully flirt. Why would I want to talk to girls when there were grown moms who were so wise nearby? It was sixth grade, and I was not a boy, not yet a man.

Not everyone is on the same body-changing schedule in the sixth grade, but I remember a thin, dark mustache sprouted within a week that fall, and my voice would fluctuate between Kristin Chenoweth on helium and Bea Arthur with a cold. Hormones were flooding through my body, and blood traveled to my bottom half like a cascading waterfall anytime I saw Brendan Fraser on the *George of the Jungle* movie poster or walked down the underwear aisle at my local Kmart, but it wasn't like I was out to anyone.

Speaking of undies, twelve is when I switched from traditional underwear to boxers. I'll never forget receiving my first pair, which felt like a rite of passage into adulthood. Mom wrapped them up as a birthday gift alongside an art kit, and when I opened them in front of my other family members, I was so embarrassed. I started blushing when I saw that they were boxers, quickly moving on to the next gift. From my reaction, you would've thought she gave me a box of dildos, but it was just one pair of cotton underwear adorned with Taz from Looney Tunes. My birthday is in October, and it would be months before I would gather the strength to actually wear those boxers. Each day I would set them out on the bed, look at them for a moment, and then go back to my Hanes tighty-whities I was used to. That winter, I finally put them on, and a whole new world opened, a world where I was unrestrained and running free like Mariah Carey in the "Butterfly" music video or Nicole Kidman after she signed her divorce papers. Those boxers were the catalyst for me discovering my body for the very first time. It wasn't just me; everyone is trying to figure out their bodies around that age, and that causes some very awkward group slumbers.

Bobby had most of the boys from our class over one night in the spring of sixth grade, well after I had started embracing my boxers and puberty. I had planned to transfer to public school the following year, so this was one of the last group events with my Catholic school buddies. Since there were so many of us, Deb and Rick let all of us sleep in their fancy basement. I felt like Ritchie Rich staying there, because their basement had carpeting and a big-screen television, while the basement I grew up in had a concrete floor, molded wood from a flood that was never properly dealt with, and my dad's old train set from the 1960s that was also covered in (probably dangerous, possibly deadly) mold. Bobby's house was suburbia goals.

The girls from our class were all having their own sleepover, so we spent most of the early evening calling them on Bobby's second phone line. I hate to keep pointing out comparisons, but my family never, ever had a second phone line. Even when we eventually got the internet, we would inevitably get kicked off our Netscape Navigator every time Aunt Joanne called to discuss Erica Kane's latest *All My Children* antics with my mom. When Napster came along, it would take weeks to download "Lady Marmalade" because the internet kept getting cut out, so I was always envious of anyone with an extra phone line that allowed them to listen to more than just Mya's verse.

Let's take a little detour...

I loved spending the night at other people's houses, particularly because they always had the good snacks like Dunkaroos or Gushers or Cheetos. We were an off-brand/generic junk food household, so we had treats with names like Cheezzzy Curlerz or Zandwich Cookiez. Lots of misspellings and "z's" in the names instead of "s's," and the mascots for those foods were always ambiguous animals that looked like they were created by whoever animated Tom Hanks in *The Polar Express*. Very creepy. I never particularly liked cereal, but none of the brands we had in our pantry even came in a box. Our Crizpy Kookiez were packaged in bags, so by the time those snacks were put together at the warehouse, delivered to the grocery store, put onto shelves, carried home, and opened for breakfast, they were dust. If we were lucky enough to get one of the generics that came with a toy like their name-brand counterparts, it was usually a stale stick of gum or a supposedly temporary tattoo of a basic shape that never washed off. I had a circle on my forearm for the entirety of third grade courtesy of Cruncherz. Anywayz, I alwayz looked forward to staying at friendz becuz they were richer and had the good stuff in their pantriez.

The girls eventually grew tired of talking to us boys on the phone, and with Deborah and Rick seemingly asleep, we had to find something else to occupy our time. If we were fifth graders, we would've built a fort out of pillows and then pretended the floor was lava, but now that we were tweens with developing bodies, we looked for something more dangerous to do as a group.

A kid named Wes suggested streaking through the neighborhood. To be clear, my body confidence in the sixth grade wasn't great (still isn't). At pool parties I felt like a wet goblin, my T-shirt was firmly on while I was in the deep end, so the idea of taking our blouses off and running around in public was not sitting right with me. I was considered "obese" from ages nine to twelve, only losing the weight earlier that fall, shortly before the aforementioned slumber party. The word *obese* is often thrown around when it isn't applicable, but I promise you that I was considered technically obese by my primary care pediatrician. When I went out for football that autumn, I was deemed too overweight to even play on the team. Most people think being heavy is a good thing when it comes to that sport, but the people in charge told me I couldn't play unless I lost fifteen pounds before the first game. This is when my food issues started, and to be honest, they've never gone away. I have a very unhealthy relationship with eating/dieting/body image, and it all stems from this time in my life—when adults analyzed my body and made decisions for me based on what the scale said. I often think about how much more I could get done in a day if my brain weren't so preoccupied thinking about food and weight.

When the streaking was suggested, I panicked. How could I get undressed in front of them when I wasn't even comfortable getting undressed by myself? I think the other kids at the sleepover just wanted to see each other naked to confirm that what was going on with their bodies was also going on with other people's bodies, so streaking at a boy's night seemed like a great place to figure all that out. It makes sense, but I personally didn't want to know what everyone's body looked like at that time; I just wanted to watch a VHS of Brandy and Whitney Houston in *Cinderella* and then get a good night's sleep so I could hang with Deb at our breakfast date the next morning.

"Shouldn't we go to bed? It's almost eleven," I pleaded to the group.

"Let's streak!" everyone countered.

My debate skills weren't what they are now, so I didn't have a whole lot of counterarguments. Plus, since it was not even 11:00 p.m., I knew we would have to find something to occupy the time until at least 1:00 a.m. because a slumber party is always considered unsuccessful if everyone goes to bed early. My dear grandma used to say I was "full of nerves," and that was certainly the case when it came to group hangs. All the other boys seemed so carefree about taking off their tops and running down the road of a northeast Ohio suburban neighborhood, but my eyes went wide, my butt clenched, and I started to sweat by the mere idea of it.

Since we were all stationed in Bobby's basement, the only direct way outside was through a window near the ceiling that opened to the backyard. In an effort to make this night as dangerous as possible, the group built a ladder made of mostly empty boxes that led to the window, and it was decided that we would each climb up the boxes, through the opening to the outside, where we would then take off our clothes, run to the stop sign and back, and then we would all jump around in the backyard without our clothes on like a bunch of giddy hippies. I can't remember who decided on this exact itinerary, but everyone agreed that it was the best order of events for a successful night. One by one, the other kids traveled up that box ladder and out the window. Wes, Ryan, and Darnell all went out and disrobed as I sat fearing for my life, with my shirt firmly on. One of the kids, Jimmy, wore a brace that night after breaking his arm playing basketball. You would think he would sit this out, as he had an extra obstacle keeping him from full nakedness. Instead, Jimmy confidently removed his brace and hopped outside for some public nudity without a care in the world. Mad props to Jimmy, but I can't imagine that's how his doctor wanted his arm to heal.

Before I knew it, it was just Bobby and me left in the basement, the only two left to get naked and run to the stop sign. Bobby hadn't hit puberty yet, but it was his house, so he knew he would have to join in even though he clearly didn't want to take off his clothes either. By waiting until all the other boys went, he figured it reduced how much time they would see his bits. We looked at each other with fear in our eyes, and at that moment, I knew I had no choice but to complete the mission.

I tossed Bobby aside and carefully climbed the box ladder before him, determined not to be the last one left in the basement. As one of the final people to go outside, I noticed the cardboard on the box ladder was starting to give in as I approached the open window that led to the Narnia of preteen nudity. My foot slipped through the top and the cardboard fell to the ground just as I shimmied through the opening and into the outdoors. There was no safely turning back. Once out the window, I courageously removed my clothes and looked at the group of nudists already outside directing me to my stop-sign goalpost. They were all dancing like a scene from *Midsommar* without the white dresses and flower crowns.

At this point, I decided to give in to the fear. My anxiety slipped away with every article of clothing I tossed to the ground. The last thing to go were the Tasmanian Devil boxers, which signified my loss of innocence as they fell to the cold, wet grass. Endorphins flowed through my body, and the excitement of something daring took hold of my emotions. The adrenaline rush of running outdoors without any fabric clinging to my body was a high I had never experienced before and have been chasing ever since. All my cares were gone as I felt the Ohio spring night breeze floating through every crevice of my newly developed frame.

I sprinted from the backyard to the front, and then the streetlamps lit the way as I reached the open road. At first, I covered my privates with my hands, but I eventually threw caution to the wind and allowed myself to feel something other than nerves for what, at the time, felt like the first time in my entire existence. My smile went wide, I screamed with glee, and flailed my arms about like those inflatables that you find outside a car dealership, all the while laughing maniacally like the Joker. "Why so serious?" I wondered about my previous demeanor. My legs didn't slow down either, they just kept running, and running, and running. Pretty soon, the excitement wore off, and my limbs started to slow from exhaustion. In my naked delirium, I had forgotten to look for the stop sign that was supposed to signal me to turn back around and rejoin the group in the backyard. I found myself *deep* into the neighborhood, in the middle of the road, and what felt like miles from where I started, without any clothing.

I looked around and didn't see any of my friends. I was naked, afraid, cold, tired, and unsure of how to get back. I blacked out for a few seconds, and as I came to, I noticed the house I was standing nervously in front of decided to turn on their porch lights. "Could they see me?" I wondered. Another nearby house opened their garage. I could hear a dog barking from another, and it felt like the entire neighborhood was waking up for a show that I had never intended to sell tickets to.

Maybe I shouldn't have screamed as I ran down the street at 11:00 p.m. I realized that although I was typically asleep by ten on a normal night, the other neighborhood occupants were likely wide awake and curious about the sounds of a pubescent boy shouting in the street without a blouse on just moments earlier. Before I could even figure out where to go or what to do, I saw a car turning onto the street and driving straight for me. I covered my bottom half as the headlights flashed on my bare skin, but I was still a naked twelve-year-old, frozen with fear. Instead of moving to the sidewalk or behind a bush, I stood motionless, wide-eyed, hoping that I would be invisible if I just didn't move and allowed the driver to swerve around me. It was a young man behind the wheel, a local high school student, with a teenage girl riding passenger.

"Move, fag!" he yelled out his window as the young lady next to him shot me that look someone makes when they smell a fart. Like a dagger to my heart. Not only was I living a nude nightmare, but now it felt like someone knew my secret. My big, gay secret. Did he know that I got giddy when I saw Tom Cruise's bare ass for a split second in *Jerry Maguire*? I was panicked and still naked, wishing I would wake up from this nightmare. More neighborhood dogs started barking, and I knew I had to find my way back before a wild (domestic) animal tracked me down. I ran like hell back from where I came, and when I reached the front yard of Bobby's house, I slipped on the dewy night grass, scraping my knee on a lone tree branch. As I got up, the motion-censored lights on Bobby's house caught my movement and turned on instantly. Rick's voice echoed in the night. "What's that?" he said to his disassociated wife as he turned on the light on the nightstand. It would've been nice for Bobby to warn me not to get caught in front of those motion lights, but sometimes you have to find out the hard way.

Detour

I'm comfortable with my sexuality these days, but that wasn't always the case. I often look back at my youth and try to find the first signs of my homosexuality. Was I gay at six? How about the first grade? When I celebrated my tenth birthday, was I...I wonder. The answer is always yes, of course, but it wasn't always clear to me. In 1996, I took my brother's VHS of *Terminator* and taped over it with *First Wives Club*, and in 2000 I burned a CD with a twelve-minute remix of JLo's "Waiting for Tonight" on it. I'm sorry to stereotype, but I can't imagine a lot of young, straight boys did the same. Hindsight is twenty-twenty, and I always felt a little different than the other kids, but I didn't quite understand it all at the time. I was enamored by *Batman & Robin*, and while my contemporaries hated the campiness of it, I told anyone who would listen that Uma Thurman deserved an Oscar for her performance. Chris O'Donnell as Robin? Overwhelming for my eyes. By the time puberty hit, it felt like I was carrying a little secret that no one else knew—not even myself. More on that later...

When I reached the backyard, I expected the rest of the group to be dancing outside in their birthday suits, but instead I found a closed window and my garments missing. I looked through the glass and could see Deborah was already in the basement with the now-fully-clothed group of students, everyone snuggled in their individual sleeping bags and pretending to go to sleep to appease the adults. I wanted to bang on the opening and say, "Let me in and give me my pants!" But I didn't know what Deb knew. I started to worry that I would have to spend the rest of the night outside, my bared caboose on the wooden swing set. Would Rick find me curled up in a dirty sandbox the next morning? With bated breath, I watched and waited for Deb to turn out the basement lights and head upstairs before I gently tapped on the glass for someone to come and let me in. The boxes were no longer there to climb down, but Bobby quietly came to my rescue, using a broomstick that his cleaning person left behind to crack open the window. I leapt inside like an off-brand Catherine Zeta-Jones in *Entrapment*. A Kathy Feta-Jimmy if you will.

"Where have you been?" Bobby asked as he handed me my clothes.

"Where have I been? WHERE HAVE I BEEN?! How long was I away?" I wondered. Time was an illusion to me that evening. I couldn't have been gone more than five minutes, but Bobby acted like I had been streaking for hours. Did I exist on a separate space-time continuum? Or was all this an elaborate prank where they bamboozled me into thinking I was gone for an eternity? I may never know.

"I...don't know where I was. I just kept running. Did your mom catch everyone naked?" I asked Bobby.

"No, everyone came in after you ran off and they put their clothes on. Mom heard us laughing and came down to tell us to go to bed," he replied.

"What was everyone laughing about?" I asked.

"Wes and Darnell planned to prank you all along. Once you were gone, they wanted to steal your clothes and lock you out of the house," Bobby said.

The only word that came to me was *wow*. Wow. The audacity. They hoodwinked me! I looked at the others, seething with a silent anger. Wes was already snoring, off to dreamland, probably plotting his next move as a suburban child villain, while I got my bearings and hoisted my Looney Tunes boxers back on. Darnell rolled his eyes at my panicked state and turned his head away, while Bobby bragged to me, explaining that he never had to take off a single article of clothing since I went out before him. Apparently, there was never even any discussion about coming to find me; they just wanted to steal my clothes and humiliate me.

"You're switching schools next year, so Wes thought you had it coming," Bobby told me.

"Wow, Bobby, wow," I replied (probably).

Have you ever bought deodorant from the drugstore? You get home, unpack it, and rest it on the bathroom counter. You go about your day, finish some errands, and then hop into the shower. You get out and dry yourself off, put on some lotion, and reach for the deodorant you bought earlier. As you lift off the cap, you instinctively apply to your underarms, and as it's reaching your body, you notice in the reflection of the mirror that it appears the deodorant has already been used before, but it's too late to stop yourself from applying. Everything happens so fast. You put it on under both arms, first the right, then the left, and then set down the applicator in confusion. You're suddenly aware that *you* never even removed the plastic protection from underneath the cap that signals its first use.

Your mind races and the only explanation is that someone used that deodorant before this moment, but it wasn't you. It was a random at the drugstore. A vagrant wandered in and reached for that same antiperspirant, only they didn't follow through with a purchase like you did; they simply removed the protective piece and applied. You feel cheated and your body feels dirty. That's how I felt at that sixth-grade sleepover.

As I saw it, those kids wanted me to freeze to death, my newly frail figure struggling to survive in the cold, Ohio evening. This was all the confirmation I needed regarding my decision to transfer to public school the following year. Just like those mean people on Twitter whose profiles are adorned with Bible verses and cross emojis despite being less-than holy when they @ people, these Catholic kids were on a one-way ticket to hell, and I was ready to party with the atheists and Jewish people in my hometown.

I didn't sleep the rest of that night. My mind was in overdrive, and I had experienced too much emotion for a twelve-year-old boy to handle. I lay in my faded, Raphael-adorned sleeping bag and stared at the ritzy, non-molded basement ceiling, thinking about my life as the hours slowly passed. Some might have admitted defeat and called their parents to pick them up, but that wasn't me, because explaining the events of that evening to my mother seemed worse than pretend-sleeping alongside my new archnemeses.

I finally heard footsteps upstairs around 6:00 a.m. It was Deb, my only ally. Knowing that she was awake and that I would have someone to talk to was healing for my overactive brain. She would inevitably tell me her problems and I would forget about my own, a comfort I treasured. I neatly folded up my blankets and tiptoed upstairs. Too much noise would wake up the others, and alone time with a mom was the only thing I had left to live for, so I was quieter than a mouse.

The experience forever changed me. As an adult, I don't worry about waking up anyone when my friends stay over my place. In fact, I'll blend some daiquiris and blast Beyoncé for all to hear as soon as my eyes open—just because I can and because I was afraid to back then around my contemporaries. It seems the ghosts of our childhoods are forever with us.

"You're up early," Deb said to me that morning as she put an extra sugar cube into an oversized mug that read, *This lady is one awesome MOM*, complete with an arrow pointing upward. The all-uppercase MOM on her coffee mug told me that this was a generic piece built on an assembly line that made countless others like it. The capitalization also told me the manufacturer simply replaced MOM with whatever noun they needed to use to sell the product. *This lady is one awesome AUNT*, another probably read. *This lady is one awesome TEACHER*, likely read another.

Lazy consumers would purchase and give it to unsuspecting loved ones. The basic personalization of Deb's prized possession made me even angrier at her husband, Rick, and her son, Bobby. I imagined Rick grabbing the mug at a gas station on his way home from an affair with a woman named Rhonda while Deb was tending to her homegrown basil. Or perhaps Bobby gave her the mug one Christmas because it was the cheapest gift he could find at the last minute. I could handle the injustice that they thrust upon me, but not the woman of the house. I wanted to tell Deb to run, to start a new life in a big city, but instead I swallowed my words as I made my way to the breakfast nook.

"I couldn't sleep," I told her.

"A lot on your mind?" she asked.

"Yeah."

"I'll pour you some extra orange juice. By the way, does your knee hurt?" Deb asked, pointing to the blades of grass that dried to my cut after my naked fall a few hours earlier.

I had completely forgotten about my scraped knee. Emotional pain has a funny way of making a physical injury seem secondary. The truth is, it did hurt, and I didn't realize until that moment because it was nothing compared to the emotional turmoil I had suffered.

"I'll be fine. It's just a bruise, but I should clean it up," I assured her as I started to walk toward the main-level restroom for some rubbing alcohol and a Band-Aid.

"If you had pants on when you were running wild, you wouldn't have scraped it," she said, finishing her sentence with a wink.

She knew. Although most people would've been horrified that someone else had been aware of their late-night streaking session,

I felt oddly comforted. I'll never know if she was eavesdropping on the conversations in the basement the night before or if she actually peaked her head out the window when she heard my naked squeals in the streets of the neighborhood where she built her family. None of that mattered, because I knew her secrets, and now she knew mine. We were equals, and none of my contemporaries who were still asleep in that basement could relate.

Without missing a beat, Deb lifted her right arm, pointing out a faint scar on the tip of her elbow. "When I was ten, I fell on my drive-way Hula-Hooping a little too hard," she said. "Some bruises last a lifetime, but they don't hurt as badly as time goes by."

Deb was right.

The Journey

Vacation: Day Zero

They say it's not about the destination, it's about the journey, but sometimes they're both awful. I've taken plenty of vacations in my day that ended up being terrible wastes of time or exhausting time sucks, and the way to those places wasn't anything special either. Sure, it's nice to be off work, but in my thirties, it feels like I'm only taking off to go to weddings, using up all my personal days to watch other people say their vows, which is not the kind of holiday I'm interested in. Crowded airports, old hotels, and expensive rideshares ensue, all for three days of celebrating a couple that will likely be divorced in eight months. Family trips aren't a walk in the park either. Growing up, Pellegrino family vacays were cursed, oftentimes before we even left the house. My parents, Gary and Linda, were the adults making the decisions about these outings, and I, along with my brothers, Junior and Bryan, went along with what they decided. Our longest trek as a family of five was from Ohio to Florida, and it was my first experience with a beautifully disastrous holiday. Cleveland to Orlando is over a thousand miles, and we did it twice in my childhood, both during the humidity-filled months of August. You would think we would have learned our lesson the first time, but my dad lives by the motto that if at first you don't succeed, do it again to be sure.

The first Florida trip took place in the summer of 1994-ish with a new car, or rather, two new cars. When it was decided that we would be driving to the Sunshine State, we needed a bigger vehicle to house our growing bodies, and so it was time Dad hit the dealerships to turn in his compact car and get something we could all fit comfortably in with luggage. He likes to keep us all on our toes and wait until the last possible moment to do anything, so the day before we were due to leave for Florida, he finally went shopping for a sturdy set of new wheels that would get us across the country.

"Get a nice, big van with one of those racks on the roof so we can mount our luggage in a cargo carrier," Mom instructed.

I thought those "turtle tops" on vehicles were so glamorous when I was growing up, when in fact, the really rich people were flying on planes, not putting a *Flintstones* duffel bag their grandma won them at a church raffle full of homemade denim shorts on the roof of a car.

"You don't get good mileage with the luggage on top," Dad replied, ignoring the rest as he went on his way.

Forever looking for a deal, Dad decided to go to a police auction instead of a traditional dealership like my mom, and anyone rational, would have done on such short notice. I've never personally been to an auction, but apparently you can get stuff at a discount when people die, or businesses close down, or items are confiscated by the local authorities. We all assumed he would arrive back with a reasonably priced new van from the showroom. Mom had us finish packing and bring our luggage to the garage so we could pack it up as soon as Dad got home. By pack, I mean I gathered my *Garfield* fanny pack, a tank that said *Designing Woven* on it that I liked only because I thought it actually said *Designing Women* on it, and my Mariah Carey cassette-filled Walkman.

Just as Mom was putting the finishing touches on dinner that night and us kids were bringing our vacation luggage into the garage, Dad arrived home with a used Chevy Caprice. It wasn't just any Chevy, it was a former cop car, stripped of any indication that it was primarily a police vehicle, except for the fact that it was EXTRA big and long. Just as we were walking our suitcases outside, Dad came driving down the road in his new, big-ass car. As he pulled into the driveway, my mom looked in horror at the sheer size of this thing, while Dad had a confident smile indicating just how proud he was of his new purchase. I can't stress enough how long this car was. Too long. Like an improv show or CVS receipt. Obviously longer than any car I had ever seen, because even my eight-year-old eyes thought it was massive. I can't imagine what kind of police work was done with this thing, as it looked like it moved at a snail's pace. Regardless, Dad rolled down the window as he eased into the driveway, slow enough to see the reaction on all four of our faces.

"Gary, what's this?" Mom inquired.

"Our new car!" Dad replied proudly.

"Where's the storage top?" I wondered.

"You said you were going to get a van, Gar! How are we all going to fit in this thing?" Mom added.

Even though it was grotesquely long, it didn't look like there was a lot of space for seating or storage, and Mom could see that.

"It's extra long. Lots of trunk space for the luggage! Plus, it was super cheap," Dad said.

"Why was it so cheap?"

"Someone died near it...or in it, just move the luggage so I can pull this thing into the garage and we can load it up," Dad said while still in the driveway.

Mom had us boys move our stuff out of the garage to make room for the new car, so I dragged my wares back inside. We lived in a modest house, with what I would say was an average-size garage. It wasn't small... It was like any of the other garages that could fit two traditional vehicles and some bikes and things. The front had cabinets that housed things like tools and old baseball gloves, plus there was a big, old barrel that had loose basketballs and Frisbees in it. All in all, it was a basic, Midwest garage that we all assumed was normal.

Dad slowly began to pull the Chevy in as my mom's eyes watched with horror.

"Can I pull up any more?" he asked as the front hood grazed against the cabinets at the front of the garage.

"No, that's as far as you can go, Dad," I told him.

I could see my dad's brows raise to the heavens as he inched toward the front wall, praying that he would have enough space for this thing. Unfortunately, like the time I tried to replicate an Ashton Kutcher look by wearing suspenders over a T-shirt...it didn't work. It's always something, isn't it? Either the new car doesn't fit in the garage, or you look more like the Mucinex booger than Ashton Kutcher.

"Gary, the car doesn't fit!" Mom said as she looked at the trunk hanging about four feet past the door and into the open driveway. The garage door would obviously not close with the butt of this thing sticking out so far.

"What do you mean it doesn't fit?" He turned the engine off and surveyed the parked car.

"You bought a car that doesn't fit in the garage, Gary!" Mom shouted, both stating the obvious and embarrassing my father in front of his three impressionable young boys.

Dad looked at the car and began to stew with anger. He always had a short fuse, so we knew the emotion that was coming, but we were less likely to have predicted the mix of words that would come out of his mouth.

"Fucking Saremba! Damnit!" Dad said.

I'm sure you're reading this and thinking, "What or who is Saremba?" I was too. My mother, of course, immediately knew who Dad was throwing the blame to and who was the recipient of his rage.

"That fucking Saremba is an idiot!" he continued.

"You were the one who bought a car that didn't fit in the garage, Gar! You said you were gonna get a nice, family van with a luggage rack," Mom reminded him, getting more and more upset herself.

"There's less mileage with luggage racks! And the car would've been fine if fucking Saremba built the fucking house right!" he exclaimed with eyes as wide as the trunk of the new-old Chevy.

Saremba was the builder of our house. No, we never once met him, but he was a prominent figure in my childhood from then on. Technically, I don't even think it was the name of a singular person, just the name of the construction business. Whenever anything would go wrong inside or around our home, Dad would say, "Fucking Saremba!" When the roof leaked because the gutters were clogged with leaves, Dad blamed fucking Saremba. When the porch swing broke after a particularly rousing thunderstorm, it was because of fucking Saremba. Saremba was the Joker to his Batman, the Burger King to his McDonald's, and the Megavolt to his Darkwing Duck. Dad hated this man with every ounce of his being, and the garage cabinets blocking the big-ass car so that it wouldn't properly close sent my dad over the edge.

"Get me my box of cigarettes," he instructed me.

Dad got back into the Chevy Caprice and quickly backed it all the way out of the garage while I fetched his value pack of smokes.

"And grab me my hammer!" he told Bryan.

"Keep your voice down; the neighbors will hear," Mom told him sternly through her teeth as voices escalated.

"Screw the neighbors!" Dad yelled from inside the vehicle as he began to unravel.

He parked the car in the driveway, grabbed his box of cigs from my child hands, and surveyed the inside of the garage.

"I'm gonna do something that fucking Saremba should've done in the first place," he said, lighting one of his Marlboro Lights, taking an aggressive drag, and gripping his hammer with a strength that would make Thor jealous.

"What are you going to do?" Mom asked.

"A garage is for cars! I'm getting rid of these cabinets so we can fit the vehicle inside as God intended," he said as he used the claw part of the hammer to swiftly rip the cabinets from the wall.

"Are you nuts? Even without the cabinets, the car still won't fit," she countered.

"Sure, it will, honey. It's a garage, and they're made to fit all sorts of vehicles."

"The car you bought is too long! It won't fit, Gar!"

By this point, it didn't matter what anyone said. Dad was already halfway to ripping down the cabinets with a frustration that can only be described as Donald Duck on Adderall or a (more) deranged Grinch. Whatever was inside of the storage began falling out. My brothers and I were gathering up the remains and trying to find new homes for the items, while my mom threw her hands up and went inside for a glass of stress wine.

This way my dad gets at times, some people call it "seeing red." With him, it's like an evil spirit takes over his body. He's since tamed tremendously and is no longer a smoker, but we grew up getting to know this part of him. He became possessed, like a chain-smoking Italian version of the Hulk, but instead of trying to save the world, he was swearing at the ghost of a man and unintentionally wrecking our home.

Dad spent the next hour ordering us around and making some more room in the garage for his new car. We repositioned the barrel of balls to the other side and dragged the dismembered cabinets to the curb for trash pickup. I thought it looked good and clean for such a quick renovation! I imagine that's how Joanna Gaines feels at the end of an episode of *Fixer Upper*. Mom, however, was horrified that the pieces of loose wood would be waiting on the curb for almost a whole week, as the city had just collected our garbage. She cooled down just enough after another glass of pinot grigio to come back out and assess the damage from the driveway, just as Dad was starting the Caprice back up to drive it into the garage for a second try.

"Danny, tell me how much room I have up front," Dad said.

I waved him forward until the car was literally touching the wall where our storage cabinets *used* to be. You could see where they once were, as it was unpainted, something that would remain so for years to come and remind us of this exact moment.

Dad put the car in park and asked, "Am I good back there?"

"No! You bought a car that doesn't fit in the garage, Gary!" Mom informed him.

Every time she reminded him that he bought a car that didn't fit in the garage, you could see his face getting redder and redder, filled with blood and rage. If he were a cartoon, a flame would've shot from his forehead and exploded in the air like Fourth of July fireworks.

The most frustrating thing was that he knew Mom was right. Most people don't consider measuring the length of the vehicle before driving it home, but if you're buying an unusually long one, perhaps you should pack a ruler. Hours prior, he was on cloud nine, proud of his purchase and excited to share the good news, but now he was about ready to explode. He couldn't get mad at his wife because she sent him off to get a reasonably sized van, and we were kids, so he couldn't yell at us for this misstep. A more emotionally mature person would have blamed himself, but not my pop. He unscrewed the lid containing his anger and let out the loudest "FUCKING SAREMBA" yet as he realized there was no way to fit this thing in the garage without doing some more extensive, wall-down renovations. Mom tried to diffuse the situation...

"Let's just postpone the vacation. I'll call the hotel and see if they can—"

"WE'RE GOING OUT OF TOWN TO RELAX, LINDA!" he replied through clenched teeth in a tone that was anything but relaxed.

The words barely left his mouth as he got back into the Caprice and floored it in reverse on his way to an actual car dealership, which is where he should've gone in the first place. He couldn't return it to the police auction, but he could trade it in at a used car lot like he had traded in the compact car we started with that morning. En route out of the driveway, he drove into one of the curbside cabinets that he ripped off the wall moments before, pummeling the loose wood into the middle of the road in front of our home and damaging the car on the way to turn it in.

Rolling down the window with a freshly lit cig in his mouth, he shouted one last message to his young family. "Get that fucking wood out of the road, I'm getting a new fucking car."

Junior and Bryan dragged the cabinet pieces back to the curb, while I followed my mom inside for moral support. She poured herself another glass of stress wine at the kitchen table, emptying the bottle, licking the rim to soak up every last drop, and whispering a Hail Mary. The thought of getting into the car with three children and the evil spirit that took over Dad's body for a family road trip was almost too much for her to handle in that moment, so despite not being a regular at church, she called on God and booze.

As Mom took a heavy swig of wine, she noticed the budget hotel confirmation number she had previously scribbled down on a stray *Sonic the Hedgehog* notepad in front of her, and she shook her head in disgust, likely thinking about all the wishes she had for the vacation week ahead. She wished she could fly instead of drive. She wished she had the money for a spacious room to share with her family instead of the cheap hotel that was booked. And her biggest wish of all was that she could go on her own vacation, putting motherhood aside for a few days to experience the type of tranquility she hadn't known since before her firstborn came along. Memories of adult trips with her girlfriends flooded her head, and she remembered the spa weekend she had with her besties in Palm Springs before she was married. Linda reminisced about the time she drank frozen daiquiris and gossiped on the beach, doing the things you're supposed to do when you're out of town and off work. The nostalgia quickly faded as she snapped back into the present. Despite my young age, I knew in that moment that I needed to go to my room and leave her alone, aware that mom needed another vacation from the pre-vacation *and* the actual vacation, just like all mothers do.

A couple of hours later, after all of us were tuckered out in our rooms for the night, Dad came home with *another* Chevy (he was convinced Chevys run better than other brands). The extra-long car from earlier, the Chevy Caprice, was a thing of the past a mere hours after it was our expected future, and Dad replaced it with an even bigger vehicle...the Chevy Astro Van. Even though this new van he got us for vacation was huge, it wasn't extraordinarily long like the other. For what was lost in length, it made up for in height. Dad was able to park the new ride in the garage without any trouble closing, and he went to bed that night at peace. Peace knowing that his wife would be pleased with the van she had originally requested, peace knowing his kids would all fit inside of it with their luggage, and peace knowing that the garage door would safely shut. He would close his eyes next to his beautiful almost-always-right wife and dream about his upcoming trip to a warm Florida beach with the family he loved. The knots of stress that developed that fateful day slowly dissipated as he drifted asleep, unaware that new stress knots would be forming very, very soon.

Vacation: Day One

With a brand-new (used) van ready to take us to Florida, the Pellegrino family finally loaded our luggage the next morning. While Mom was happy it was big and still fit in the garage, it didn't have the fancy rack on top for bags like she hoped for, so we had to carefully Tetris our stuff in the trunk in order for everything to fit. Dad and Bryan prided themselves in utilizing the space to the best of their abilities, and somehow, they got all the sausage into the casing.

If you've never been inside an Astro van, you should know that there are usually three rows of seats—the driver/passenger, then two other rows in the back. For ours, the middle row of seats was removed before we even hit the road so that we could put pillows and blankets down and sleep on the way. In retrospect, this was possibly illegal and certainly not safe.

With no proper seating in the back, at any given moment on the ride to Florida, there were three people shuffling around the floor of a van without a seat belt or anything to keep them in place. Whenever we hit a speed bump, my tiny child body would fly to the air like I was on a traveling trampoline. Dad thought he was doing us a solid after the Caprice debacle by giving us extra space to sprawl out, but maybe we should've had actual seats with seat belts. Nowadays it seems like kids use car seats well into their teens, but we didn't adhere to those restrictions in the '90s.

Not only did Dad get us the big-ass van and not make us wear seat belts, but he also bought a tiny television set with a VCR attached. Kids today don't understand how high tech this was. Watching movies in a moving vehicle wasn't commonplace. This was years before the headrests turned into DVD players or cell phones could play episodes of *Euphoria*, and we thought it was VERY luxe to sit on the floor of our new van and watch a movie on a four-inch screen while my loving maniac of a father got us to Orlando.

The movies we brought along were family favorites on VHS like *My Cousin Vinny*, *Sister Act*, *Sister Act 2*, and *Planes, Trains, and Automobiles*. *My Cousin Vinny* isn't exactly family-friendly, but it was my dad's fave, and Marisa Tomei made my mom laugh, so she allowed it. Ms. Tomei rightfully won the Academy Award for her performance, and the scene where she talks about the pants Vinny is wearing to shoot deer is one of the greatest comedic scenes of all time, but I digress. There are a lot of f-bombs in the movie but no more than my dad used when talking about the man who built our house, whom he didn't even know personally, so in the words of the legendary Irish girl group B*Witched, c'est la vie.

My parents didn't believe in staying anywhere overnight along the way since it was more costly, so we drove the entire distance, only stopping for food and gas, even though no one else other than my dad was equipped to drive. Mom refused because it was a big-ass Astro van without seat belts for her children, and my brothers weren't old enough to drive yet, so that meant Dad was behind the wheel for eigh-teen plus hours...or so we thought. Whenever I see family road trips in movies, the wife is riding passenger, but Linda was not interested in even being up front acting as the human navigation. She wanted to lie in back and nap in between viewings of the *Sister Act* films. No one can resist the charms of Whoopi Goldberg and Kathy Najimy singing in habits. Bryan was the most obedient of us, so Dad convinced him to help direct him while riding passenger. Back then there was no Google Maps or MapQuest or TomTom, so Bryan had a giant paper map that was bigger than he was. If you asked me to use that thing, even now, I would lead you to the Emerald City, not Florida. When I see a map, all my critical thinking skills go out the window and I feel like I'm looking at one of those magic eye layouts you used to see in the Sunday news-paper. My brain simply cannot compute a map of any kind. Dad also had a fancy radar detector that was supposed to beep every time we were near the police so he could slow down and drive the speed limit, but that soon went to shit. About an hour into the drive, it wouldn't stop beeping, so Dad threw it out the window and Bryan had to act as a Foley artist, making noises if he saw a speed gun or anything that resembled the car that didn't fit in our garage the night before.

During the middle-of-the-night driving, the TV went off and Mom, Junior, and I went to sleep, while Dad and Bryan kept us on schedule. I know I said my Dad was piloting for eighteen plus hours, but it's time I live my truth. I have a vivid memory of that specific road trip that comes to me at random like a *That's So Raven* vision. Sometimes I'll see this in my sleep, and other times it will come to me when I'm in line at the grocery or working out at the gym. It was the wee hours and everyone in back was snoozing. The car swerved, and my tiny body slid across the floor of the van, abruptly waking me up. My eyes opened and I wondered if we had arrived in Florida. I soon realized I was still in the van, and we were on a quiet road, most likely somewhere outside of Georgia. I heard a familiar snoring, but Mom and Junior were both quiet sleepers, so I knew it wasn't them. This was the loud snore of a grown man. I glanced at the dashboard to look at the time. I rubbed my eyes to see more clearly, but I still couldn't make out the digits on the clock, so I grabbed my glasses and put them on to see that it was just after 3:00 a.m. The loud snores came from up front, so with my corrected vision, I looked at the culprit in the passenger seat...it was Dad! So, by now you're probably wondering who was driving. I was too. Mom was passed out, and the rest of us were fourteen and under. Before I could do the math, I heard my twelve-year-old brother...

"Go to sleep, Danny!"

Bryan was behind the wheel, with Mom and Dad off in dreamland.

"Why are you driving?" I asked him in a whisper.

It was a simple, innocuous question, but Bryan acted like I asked him something absurd. I might as well have said, "Why are you dressed like Ursula the Sea Witch?" or "Are you the Zodiac Killer?" I thought my question was valid and straightforward, but Bryan was wildly offended and simply wanted to continue his journey of being in charge of our collective journey.

"Dad was teaching me how to drive, now shut up and go back to bed!"

"But Dad's asleep," I replied.

"You should be too!" Bryan instructed.

"But—"

My line of questioning was distracting him from the task at hand, and he briefly found himself driving on the wrong side of the road. He swerved to get us back on track, and fortunately (or unfortunately), the sudden movement didn't wake up any of the others, although Dad shifted a bit in the passenger.

"Go back to sleep, you're annoying me!" he exclaimed.

Rather than argue, I followed his instructions and curled back up with my blanket. Years before Carrie Underwood rose to fame courtesy of *American Idol*, I lay back down and I too called for Jesus to take the wheel as I closed my eyes on a midnight Astro van through Georgia. I'm not sure why I was so comfortable sleeping when my life was in the hands of a tween who hadn't even hit puberty, but I drifted off to bed and my eyes wouldn't reopen until the next morning.

The sun rose and I, too, began to awaken. As I put my glasses on again, I saw that Dad was back in the driver's seat as if nothing had happened. Was I dreaming? How long was my twelve-year-old brother leading us to Florida? I may never know. Mom couldn't believe how chipper Dad was the next day, and they were laughing and making cute jokes with each other all morning as we entered the Florida state limits.

"Normally you're cranky if you don't get enough sleep," I overheard Mom say to Dad.

"Vacation is all about relaxing," he said calmly as if he'd unlocked the secret to a successful trip.

"It must've been a bumpy road because I felt like I rocked to sleep," she said. What she didn't know is that the rockiness was due to her middle child being barely able to see the road and reach the pedal at the same time without almost driving us into a ditch. And Dad was only happy because he'd gotten a few solid hours of z's. Bryan, on the other hand, was grumpier than usual. Instead of sleeping like the rest of us, he drove from Savannah to Jacksonville without any conscious company, and when Dad finally did come to, Bryan was forced to direct him again *and* keep an eye out for the po-po.

When we finally arrived at our destination, Mom and Dad instructed us to stay in the car while they checked us in at the hotel office. The vacation property was set up differently than a traditional resort. There was an office in one location, and down the road, in a separate building, were the rooms that the guests stayed in. Us kids watched as they got the keys from the rental office, anxiously awaiting the moment we could get out of the godforsaken van we had spent so many hours in. Despite having extra leg room without the middle row of seats, it wasn't like we were in a spacious camper. It was still four males and one adult female in a van for the length of the time it would take to watch the entire *The Lord of the Rings* extended edition saga, plus *The Irishman* and a Judd Apatow feature.

The parents came back to the vehicle from the check-in office holding our room key and a flowerpot with a gator and flamingo holding hands on it, which Mom gripped proudly. The check-in office had a little gift shop and she saw a pot she liked quite a bit, so she splurged and bought it, declaring the pot her first souvenir. She had a wide smile on her face, and while it might not have seemed like much, purchasing it was her way of starting the trip off with a splurge. The night prior was so chaotic, and the drive so long, she wanted to treat herself now that she assumed the fun part of the vacation was about to start.

The rooms were a few blocks away from the check-in center, so we had to drive just a little bit more. Once we arrived in our designated parking spot, Dad opened the back of the van and started to unpack the luggage immediately, even before checking out our new digs. The baggage had fit perfectly in the van, so emptying became a strategic game to ensure things didn't fall out willy-nilly. All the bags came out one by one, and we sat them outside the car so it would be easy for all of us to take everything inside, like a family-style assemble line.

Just as we got the last of the gear out of the trunk, we heard a scream. Mom noticed the window of our hotel room was shattered, looking like someone had broken in, so we wouldn't be staying there after all. That meant the belongings my dad just carefully unloaded would now have to return to the trunk.

"Damn it," Dad said, this time unable to blame the events on Saremba.

Packing the van the first time not only took him about an hour, but it also took a lot of concentration. He was lacking the patience and demeanor to do it for a second time after such a long road trip. He was trying his best to remain calm, but his patience wouldn't last long. The bigger bags went in, and he tried to position everything else the way it was before the broken hotel window reveal. He'd ask us boys to hand him others to speed up the process, but with only half the goods in and the trunk seemingly already full, there was no way he was packing it as efficiently as he did the first time.

"Should've gotten the cargo carrier," Mom said under her breath but purposefully loud enough for everyone to hear.

Dad pulled everything out of the trunk again and started over, his temper now flaring as he tried to repack the luggage of five people. Ordinarily he would've reached for a smoke, but mom wouldn't let him pack his cigarettes on the trip, encouraging him to quit over the relaxing vacation. Oops.

"Get in the van, I'll load it myself," he told us.

We all knew that meant everyone except Bryan should go back into the vehicle. Junior and I got out of a lot of manual labor throughout the years because we weren't quite as obedient. He and I are both more stubborn than Bryan is, so our middle brother got stuck being Dad's right-hand man, even when he was running on zero sleep. My mom set down her new flowerpot alongside the luggage outside the van and then settled in while Dad and Bryan took care of it. I continued to watch them through the window as they tried to fit everything, this time seemingly finding more success than the last effort, and pretty soon everything was loaded in other than my mom's new souvenir flowerpot. I watched as Bryan handed it to Dad to pack in, but without missing a beat, Dad tossed it into a nearby trash can, shattering it to pieces before he slammed the trunk closed and got back in the driver's seat.

"I threw away your ceramic tub," he announced glibly as he put the keys into the ignition, not thinking it was of any real importance.

"My what?" Mom asked.

"The tub!"

"What tub?"

"Your ceramic tub!"

"A bathtub?"

"Your plant tub!"

"What's a plant tub?"

"Your tub, your tub, the fucking tub!" Dad said, surely wishing he had a Marlboro to calm his nerves.

When Dad got this upset, he didn't make any sense. Part of me thinks my mom liked to rile him up by acting clueless just to get under his skin. It always worked and I find myself using this tactic to piss off people in my own adult life. It's one of the most fun ways to annoy people.

"I don't know what you're talking about."

"Your ceramic plant tub!" he yelled.

"My flowerpot?" she asked.

"Yes, I threw it away."

"Why are you calling it a ceramic tub, Gar?"

"That's what it is!"

"It's a flowerpot!"

"Same thing!"

"Turn back around, I want to go get it."

"It's broken. I threw it in the trash can."

"Gary! I just bought it!"

"We don't have room for it."

"You should've gotten a van with a cargo carrier like I said," Mom told him.

"Mom's always right!" I added.

"Do you want to go back home, because I'll drive us right back to Ohio!" Dad replied.

Bryan's eyes went wide as soon as this threat left my father's mouth. He worried that he'd have to take the wheel, and he wasn't ready for that kind of responsibility quite so quickly after his last late-night drive.

"If you would've gotten the cargo carrier, we could've put our souvenirs in the trunk," Mom said.

"We don't need any souvenirs! We have enough shit at home," Dad countered.

"It was cute!"

"Flamingos and gators aren't friends, Lin!"

"I'll buy my souvenirs if I want to buy my souvenirs. You're buying cars left and right..."

"This is a van, not a car!"

"You bought that other car! You got this van and that other one that—"

The words were coming out of her mouth, and even she knew that what she was about to say was going to push him over the edge, but she didn't care. She wanted this man to know that she was right and he was wrong. If he had put his ego aside and listened to her in the first place, then maybe we all wouldn't be in this mess.

"Don't say it—" Dad pleaded.

"You bought that other car...that didn't fit in the garage."

Silence. He hung his head in shame as the air went out of Dad's metaphorical tires and he finally had to accept defeat.

No one else said a word as we pulled back into the hotel check-in office parking lot, ready to exchange the keys and get a new room. Dad went in while Mom waited in the van with us, arms crossed and no stress wine for her to grab hold of. After a few minutes, he exited the office with a pamphlet and a brand-new flowerpot, only this pot was bigger and shinier than the one that was shattered near our previously booked room, albeit without the animals on it. He entered the van and handed it to Mom in the back seat without saying a word, and she didn't say anything either, just shooting him a look. I learned in that moment that two people in a marriage can say so much without saying anything at all. Mom looked out the window as she held her new pot, and we exited the lot in the Astro van, a van that already created a lifetime of memories.

I assumed Dad booked us a new room at the same hotel, but I was wrong. Instead we hit the open road. Dad glanced at his pamphlet while the rest of us sat exhausted at what was the start of our family trip, quietly looking out the windows and wondering how we would all survive the next few days with each other. A few minutes later, we pulled into a resort that looked way chicer than that other place we were planning to stay.

"It says they have HBO in the rooms!" I shouted as I saw the sign outside, excited to spend my nights watching *Don't Tell Mom the Babysitter's Dead* like everyone else who had premium cable did in the '90s.

"Looks like we'll have HBO this week," Dad assured.

When he went into the original hotel office, he canceled our reservation and made a new one. He splurged for a nicer hotel without running it by any of us. It probably cost more than he wanted, and who knows if he was fully refunded for the last place, but it was his way of apologizing. The new hotel had a pool, a bar, and a much bigger souvenir shop in the lobby, filled with all sorts of items no one needs but will buy anyway because that's what you do on vacations; you buy expensive souvenirs that remind you that you're supposed to treat yourself. It was the kind of hotel Mom had wished she was staying at twenty-four hours earlier when she was making her wishes. She got out of the van with a confident smile on her face and a new flamingo-less flowerpot in her hands. It wasn't the spa getaway she daydreamed about being on with her friends, and it certainly wasn't a relaxing few days, but at least she got a room upgrade and only had a few days left. Mom looked at the family she loved more than anything—the kids who were already exhausted and the husband she so carefully chose to spend the rest of her life with, and she realized that a family vacation isn't about having fun or recharging your batteries, it's about finding the little victories on the way to the finish line. It's about getting through the journey alongside the ones you love.

Sadness Unfelt

There's an e e cummings poem titled "I Carry Your Heart" that I first heard in the 2005 Cameron Diaz/Toni Collette (underrated) movie *In Her Shoes*. It's a beautiful piece that I interpret differently every time I hear or read it, like the best art always asks you to do. In many ways, it encapsulates what this entire existence and ride is all about—we go through life carrying the hearts of those who mean the most to us, becoming a collection of the best (and sometimes worst) of those people. In putting this book together, I thought not just about the stories I wanted to share but also about what I wanted to say, which are two very different things. First and foremost, I hope you find a good laugh somewhere in these pages, but I also hope you take some things beyond the read, by carrying a little piece of me with you.

My grandmother and I were very close when she was alive. She was an angel and I still find myself thinking of her daily. Grandma P. would look after me in the afternoons when my mom was working. We would watch *The Rosie O'Donnell Show* or reruns of *The Golden Girls* together before driving to pick up my grandfather from work. As

I got older, we still managed to find time to spend with each other, but it dwindled. She didn't have a lot of money, but she always made an effort to make those outings special, collecting coupons in an envelope and letting me choose which one we would use for our lunch dates. Even throughout college, I would come home for holidays and we would browse the envelope for a cheap meal that was just an excuse to spend time together. We were family, but we were also buddies.

My ambition took me to Chicago after college, and later California. Grandma started to get sick when I moved to the West Coast. We would talk on the phone, and each time her voice would be weaker and weaker as she courageously battled cancer.

"Do you want me to try to come home?" I'd ask.

"No, I'm fine, you have to stay there and become a big star," she'd say quietly into the phone as someone held it close to her mouth.

Our calls got shorter and shorter as time went on, often interrupted by another family member or nurse who would tell me she was too tired to talk. I'd feel a tinge of guilt about not being there that I was able to quickly talk myself out of, thinking I was doing what was best for me by building a new life.

Eventually the call that I was dreading came; it was my dad telling me that she passed. My heart broke as I searched online for budget flights back to Ohio.

"Keep it together," I would tell myself to try to stop the tears in front of my then-roommate. I've always been comfortable crying but not so much when it was in front of other people.

A few days prior to her passing, I met a guy, we'll call him Josh, at the bookstore that I used to frequent, and he asked me on a date.

When we met, he was working on what I thought was poetry but was actually a class from a scammy online college where the diploma is just an email that says, "You're done." He wore casually sexy glasses and drank a tall, iced coffee, muscles bursting out of his short-sleeved button-down shirt. Josh was sexy-smart in a Clark Kent kind of way, looked very rich, and I was convinced he was the man I was going to marry. Rather than cancel on him, I thought I'd fly out a night later, which would also save me some money and allow me to get to know the man that I was convinced would father my children.

Detour

It makes me sad that bookstores are becoming more and more obsolete. I spent years working at a Borders book retailer in Solon, Ohio, and before that I used to spend afternoons in the shop reading *Men's Health*, staring at the shirtless men within the pages and eventually discovering that the establishment also carried adult mags. Not only that, but they had an "Alternative Interests" section, filled with all the gay books you could imagine (and also vegan cookbooks because being vegan in the Midwest was considered an alternative lifestyle back then). I would grab hold of the more traditional publications like *USA Today*, *Entertainment Weekly*, and *People* before snagging a *Playgirl* and whatever alternative lifestyle books I could find. I'd then hide all the gayest stuff underneath my copy of *USA Today* before retreating to the corner of the coffee shop to look at the topless men and read about gay culture. It felt like a new world was opening up to me, like the first time walking into a Hot Topic after listening to Evanescence. Stories of worldly homosexuals filled the pages I read and I began to dream of a life living in a big city surrounded by good-looking men in high-end clothes, with Starbucks coffee and diverse friends (Tom Hanks and Meg Ryan's *You've Got Mail* also inspired these dreams). These books were my only view of the outside world at the time—an insight into the possibility of being confident, successful, and gay. I'm forever grateful for bookstores for showing me that a world such as that existed.

"Am I being insensitive?" I asked my roommate.

"No, it will be good to get your mind off things. Go out with the guy and have fun," she encouraged.

I decided to keep our date and crossed my fingers that the emotions of my grandmother's passing wouldn't spill out with him. I was wrong.

Josh didn't tell me what the plans were, and since he asked me out, I assumed he would take care of all that. I wanted to play it cool, so I didn't ask many questions, simply put on my hottest outfit (hand-me-down True Religion jeans that were a size too small and the only sweater I owned that cost more than thirty-five dollars) and waited for him to pick me up. He arrived twenty-three minutes late in his brand-new BMW, freshly cleaned, and no longer wearing his sexy glasses yet somehow looking even sexier without.

"Where are we headed?" I asked, pretending I hadn't been waiting outside my apartment building for twenty-two minutes while looking at old pictures of my grandma on my phone.

"I thought we'd do dinner and maybe get some ice cream for dessert," he replied.

My grief now seemed a distant memory with the sight of Josh with his beautifully big thighs and new car. They say the best way to get over someone is to get under someone new, so I was ready to get under Josh and forget about my nana. Maybe that's not exactly what that phrase was about, but carpe diem. Anyway, seeing him in person reminded me that everything about him exuded wealth, so my only concern was that I would be underdressed for dinner. I started to worry he was out of my league.

Josh was one of those insane drivers who will make you fear for your life, so once we drove out of my building's parking lot, I was silently praying that I wouldn't be joining my grandma anytime soon in the afterlife. I'm terrible behind the wheel, but there's a big difference between terrible and maniacal. He drove at least 20 miles per hour over the speed limit the entire way, ran stop signs, red lights, and overall just made me feel like I was in the passenger seat of Luigi's car on Rainbow Road. Still, part of me found it extremely hot that he was so reckless (I was young and naive), while the other part of me was concerned we wouldn't make it to dinner because we would get pulled over or someone would hit us with a red turtle shell.

We eventually did arrive...at the parking lot of a strip mall.

"Are we picking up something before dinner?" I asked, assuming maybe he had to run into the drugstore.

"No, we're here," he said.

I looked around and saw no establishments that looked like where I imagined we would go on our first dinner date. There was a Walgreens, a karate dojo, and a fast food restaurant that served Americanized Mexican food. Certainly he wasn't taking me to a chain restaurant where you seat yourself...right? I thought maybe he would escort me into the karate dojo, where a picnic would be awaiting us; instead we walked into the place that had a drive-through attached.

Let me remind you all that I'm not someone who expects a lot, and I can appreciate dining modestly (I ride hard for Arby's), but this man had a BMW and, I'd find out later, a platinum Amex, so shouldn't we have been eating steak and diamonds instead of $0.79 tacos? We waited in line to order, and my whole life flashed before my eyes. I had already felt so bad about not being with my grandma before she passed, and now I was sacrificing being with my family in a time of mourning to eat at a place that gave off-brand *Hot Wheels* toys with the kids' meals. Just as I considered running for the door and catching a cab home, I noticed that his shirt lifted a bit near his belt buckle, and he had one of those protruding veins right where the top of his pubic hair peaked out. It was enough to encourage me to ignore the red flags and enjoy a fountain Diet Coke.

"Can I take your order?" the cashier asked as we reached the front of the line.

"You go ahead," I said to Josh.

"No, no, you go, I'm still looking," he insisted.

I ordered a salad, a small drink, and then turned my head to look back toward Josh.

"Go ahead and check out, I'll order separately," he said.

This was it, a step too far. Now, I was livid. When I turned my head toward him, I was expecting him to swoop in, order his own meal, and then whip out that platinum card to pay...for BOTH OF US. Instead, I had to pay for my own meal. Without getting too far into gay dating etiquette, let me just say that he was the one who asked me out, so therefore I expected him to pay. I mean, that's universal manners! I knew he had the money, but even if he didn't, I would've been MORE than happy to do a non-dinner date or spend the night at one of our apartments, where I would recommend renting a Marvel movie on demand and then "accidentally" rent *Something's Gotta Give* instead. And if I was the one who asked him out, I would've been sure to take him somewhere I could afford to pay for both of us. None of his plan sat right with me. Maybe Countess Luann is right, elegance IS learned (*my friends*).

And yet still, I pressed on, waiting for the employee to set my $3.99 salad on top of the plastic lunch tray that they served their meals on so I could find us a table that didn't wobble. My order was up first, so I grabbed the only open seating I could find, which was right next to the pour-your-own-salsa bar. Josh eventually joined me with his burrito, and in between pleasantries, other patrons would come and fill up their plastic cups of six different kinds of salsa that all looked like they hadn't been refreshed since the lunch shift.

After just a few bites of his meal, Josh excused himself to the restroom. As I sat alone, I heard Madonna's "La Isla Bonita" playing softly on the loudspeaker. The second verse hit, I looked around me at the families gathered for an affordable meal, and the sadness of the Pellegrino grand matriarch passing washed over me. Tears flooded out into my free side of tortilla chips as I grabbed as many paper napkins as I could to stop the outward sorrow, once again reminding myself to pull it together before someone saw me sobbing to a Madonna ballad. Fast food joints aren't known for their soft linens, so the more

I dabbed, the redder my eyes got. I was able to stop the tears and compose myself moments before Josh returned and Madge finished her song.

"Everything okay?" he asked, noticing that my eyes were now devil red from the harsh recycled materials of the cheapest napkins ever made.

"Allergies," I lied, worried he might feel uncomfortable if he knew what I was actually feeling.

"Your eyes look like shit," he added.

"It must be the pollen or something," I said, brushing off his rude comment as if it were nothing, even though it emphasized my pain.

We spent the rest of the meal in silence, and we opted not to get dessert. By all accounts, this man was an asshole, but I still worried about *him* being inconvenienced by my sadness. As his beamer pulled back into my apartment building's parking lot to drop me off, he put it in park and leaned in for a kiss.

"That's okay," I said as I gently pushed his lips away. Burrito breath aside, I just wasn't feeling this man anymore. My standards may have been basement level, but they did exist.

Josh drove off, and I went into my apartment to start packing for my real home, wishing I could teleport to Ohio instead of taking a four-and-a-half-hour plane ride. The travel time did end up coming in handy, as I wrote a tribute to my grandma that would ultimately become her eulogy.

After the funeral services, I got a text from Josh asking to see me again. I was so emotionally raw that I finally allowed myself to be honest with my feelings, and I texted him a GIF of Teresa Giudice from *The Real Housewives of New Jersey* angrily flipping a table, then I went right back to stuffing all that emotion inside. We're often told that it's okay to grieve when someone you love dies, but not for too long. A couple days seems to be socially acceptable, but any more than that and people worry, so we bite our tongues and wait for it to come out at a later date, which is exactly what happened on that date.

Years went by, and that guilt and sadness about not being with my grandma toward the end of her life stayed within me, flaring up at random when I'd see episodes of *The Golden Girls*, or when I'd hear "Danny Boy," a song she used to sing to me as a young kid. Every year on my birthday, she would buy me a lottery ticket, the numbers strategically chosen by her, each with specific meaning. I couldn't even buy a scratch-off without thinking of her, the memory of her passing, and the guilt I felt. Each time I felt this sorrow again, I would push the despair down and try to remember the good times, reminding myself to keep it together, never allowing the tears to surface, even just a few like when I was on that wretched date, and especially not when anyone else was near me. After all, I wouldn't want to make anyone around me feel awkward.

In 2020, I had Theresa Caputo—also known as the *Long Island Medium*, a woman who connects with spirits—on my podcast. I prepped for the interview by researching her work and seeing a couple readings she did on YouTube. I wrote questions down about when she started her business and what she was like as a child, never expecting my own past or deceased relatives to come up in conversation for my podcast. When it came time to sit down with her over Zoom, I was skeptical of her talents, while also being excited to chat. As the talk went on, she began to do a reading on me, culminating in what she described as my grandmother being present with us virtually.

Simply mentioning my grandma's death caused tears to run down my face like a faucet. My inner voice was telling me to pretend I was okay like I always did, but I had no control this time. I wanted to stop the conversation, gather my thoughts, and pivot back to the medium's life and career so she didn't feel weird, but instead I was frozen in my sadness. Just like that, those emotions I had stuffed down came bubbling up to the surface, and when I finished crying, I felt a catharsis unlike anything I'd ever experienced before. I understand that everyone feels differently regarding Theresa Caputo and her work, but I am forever grateful for that moment, when I realized that some of my deepest, darkest pain was there, dormant like the cancer my grandmother was ultimately unable to fight off. It clicked: I'll always regret not flying home to be with her, but at least now I can go forward knowing that it's okay to face that regret head on, regardless of when I feel it. We can't change the past, but we can change how we act in the future.

Writing this book has been its own catharsis, digging up feelings I had forgotten about and emotions I never properly dealt with. I'm sure I'll continue to stuff everything inside and ignore it from time to time, but I know now that they will eventually come bubbling up, and that's okay. I'm no longer a stranger to the heavy pour of tears moving south on my cheeks. I often joke about how my favorite place to cry is in the shower because there's something so freeing about the water mixing with tears in a steady rainfall, unsure which is which. When the tears came that night of my fast food date, I tried to stop them. A decade later, when the crying started over a Zoom interview, I again tried to stop them because I was conditioned to hold my emotions in. Turns out the *Trolls* soundtrack was right, you can't stop the feeling. I know now that this is an issue bigger than the memory of my grandma. It's about all the sorrow we conceal for the convenience of other people.

What if we allowed ourselves to feel *whatever* came our way, *whenever* it came our way, while prioritizing ourselves over the potential awkwardness that the humans around us might face if we do? Would we be less apt to bury it inside our bodies? And the unfinished grief that is already six feet under, how can we dig it up to process it properly? Because I know that only when we release those feelings will we have room inside ourselves for all the other stuff, the good stuff.

The deepest secret about me that no one knows is that I not only carry the hearts of my loved ones like e e cummings so eloquently wrote all those years ago, but I also too often carry the burden of my sadness unfelt. Unprocessed grief is the worst sort, and writing this is a reminder to give myself the permission to feel everything when I feel it and free my body from the weight of my disregarded emotions. I hope you will join me.

Cootie Catcher

"Maybe there won't be marriage, maybe there won't be sex, but by God there'll be dancing."

MY BEST FRIEND'S WEDDING (1997)

Coming out is, I hope, much easier now than it was even just ten or fifteen years ago when I did it, just as it was easier for me than the older generations of gay men. I consider my *official* out-of-the-closet moment to be Thanksgiving weekend 2009. I was living in Chicago and dating men—specifically a cute cowboy I started throwing around *I love you*s with—so when I went back to Ohio for turkey and family time, I sat everyone down for a dramatic monologue on the Monday after the big dinner to let them know. Dad was easygoing about it, Mom struggled a bit more to accept it, but everyone came around and supported me over time. The cowboy and I didn't work out, but I'll be forever grateful that he gave me the push I needed to be honest with my family. I'll never forget that it was raining that November day and I had to pick up something from a nearby Walmart. When I arrived and got out of my parent's car sans umbrella, I stuck my arms out and had a moment with the rain, washing away the pain of living inauthentically for so long. My shoulders felt lighter than they had in years, and I smiled knowing I was finally in my truth. I felt like Tim Robbins on *The Shawshank Redemption* poster, but in reality I probably looked like Danny DeVito as the Penguin floating in water at the end of *Batman Returns*. Regardless, it was a cathartic moment.

Most gay men I know have multiple coming out moments. There's the family convo, the time you tell your closest friends, and, of course, the moment you sneak your first same-sex kiss. My first kiss with a man was in Myrtle Beach, South Carolina, when I was eighteen on a spring break trip with friends. Technically, he was the first person I ever voluntarily came out to (via my tongue in his mouth), but after that I went back in the closet and tried to date women until I was ready to admit to myself and my loved ones that I am attracted to men.

All these coming outs were emotional for me, but there's one moment with a friend that forever sticks out as the most impactful. It's not a time I chose to disclose my sexuality. Unfortunately, it was a time I was abruptly outed.

My friend Anna invited me over to her house to hang in middle school. We were buddies, and I tended to gravitate toward friendships with girls in school over the boys. After my traumatic and humiliating streaking sleepover, I wasn't interested in hanging with guys on a platonic level. Plus, the girls did all the fun stuff. I wanted to play M.A.S.H. or FLAME and talk about movies like *The Parent Trap* and *Practical Magic*. Twelve is hard enough, but it's made easier when you can be around people who have similar interests.

Anna invited me over and into her bedroom, where we decided to make one of those cootie catchers. If you're not familiar, those are the little paper fortune tellers that you fold up a bunch of different ways. Parts are labeled with colors and others with numbers, and the inside has predictions or messages written on them. Anna made one that she would use on me, and I made one to use on her, and we were convinced they would forecast our future. I wrote silly predictions about money and boys in our class. When we were all done crafting, I put my index fingers and thumbs in mine and asked Anna to first pick a color out of the four listed on the top of my cootie catcher.

COOTIE
CATCHER →

"Red," she said.

"R-E-D, red," I repeated, moving my fingers as I called out each letter so that the paper fortune teller showed numbers.

"Pick a number," I instructed.

"Two"

"One, two," I counted, again rhythmically moving my folded paper.

"Now pick another number," I said, knowing that her choice now would be the fortune that she received.

"One," she told me.

I unfolded the flap that was labeled one and read, "You will find lots of money in the near future."

"Omigod, I'm gonna be rich!" Anna exclaimed.

"Now I wanna do it!" I said to Anna, ready for her to grab the cootie catcher she made.

Just as she put her fingers in it, there was a knock at her bedroom door. It was her dad.

"Hi, Danny," Mr. Burles said.

"Hi, Mr. Burles!"

"Anna, I'm sorry, but no boys in the bedroom," he told his daughter.

"But—"

Before Anna could finish her sentence, Mr. Burles looked me up and down, noticing the pink and purple crayons I used on my origami. He saw the limp of my wrist and asked...

"You made that yourself, Danny?"

"Yeah, it's a cootie catcher," I told him.

"Maybe it's okay for you two to hang out in here. Have fun," he said as he began walking out the door, assuming I wouldn't be making a pass at his daughter.

"Wait, Mr. Burles? Do you know if the Cavs won their game tonight?" I asked before he walked out the door.

He paused and then slowly turned his head in my direction.

"You like basketball, Danny?"

"I do love to watch basketball!"

Mr. Burles turned back around and said, "You know what? I think I'll hang in here for a few more minutes."

Anna's dad pulled up the only seat at his disposal, one of those inflatable chairs that were all the rage in the late '90s and early 2000s. If you had anything sharp on you, you were fucked, but they looked cute and they were see-through. Not sure why we needed to see through our furniture, but I digress.

"Omigod, we should do my dad's fortune!" Anna said.

"How does that work?" he asked.

"You'll do great, Mr. Burles. First pick a color," I instructed as I put my hands back into my cootie catcher.

"Blue."

"B-L-U-E," I repeated.

"Now pick a number."

"Six."

"One, two, three, four, five, six. Now pick another number," I said.

"Four," he replied.

"Omigod!" I said as I lifted the flap to reveal Mr. Burles's fortune.

"What does it say?" he asked.

"It says be careful who you trust because someone is going to trick you tonight," I replied.

His eyes furrowed as anger washed over him. He felt bamboozled.

"Someone is trying to trick *me*?! Okay, Danny, you need to leave. No boys in Anna's room," Mr. Burles said sternly as he got back up and headed for the door.

Anna looked so disappointed, and I was too. I knew her dad was just being protective, but I wasn't a threat like the other boys who might have spent time at their house trying to make out with his daughter. I just wanted to hang out.

"Fine, I'll pack up my stuff and get out of here," I said.

"Let Danny stay! We're having fun!" Anna shouted back at her father, hoping to convince him to let me stay.

"No boys in your room. You two can go play in the basement or the living room," he said.

"But Dad, you let Cousin Marc play in my room."

"He's your cousin and he's... No other boys in your room, Anna."

"But Danny is...just like Cousin Marc," she replied.

At this point, I had no clue what exactly they were referring to regarding this alleged Cousin Marc, but I did sense something off about the coded language these two were speaking right in front of me, and it felt very uncomfortable. What did Anna mean when she said her cousin Marc was just like me? Was cousin Marc Italian? Was he tall like I was?

"He's...just like Cousin Marc?" Mr. Burles asked his daughter.

Anna explained, "Yeah, I think so. Danny likes basketball, but he also likes M.A.S.H. and plays with my Polly Pockets."

"I like all sorts of stuff," I told them, finally speaking up for myself, feeling like I suddenly needed to defend myself for enjoying the simple pleasures of a Polly Pocket.

Mr. Burles looked so confused and not quite ready to give up on his quest to figure me out.

"How about I hang out with you both for just a few more minutes? I can try to read Danny's fortune," he said as he sat back down on the balloon that was Anna's bedroom furniture.

Anna handed him the origami she made, and he placed his index finger and thumb inside and looked me dead in the eyes.

"Pick a color," he said with the kind of intensity usually reserved for interrogations.

"Green," I said.

"G-R-E-E-N," Mr. Burles said, suddenly an expert in cootie catching.

"Pick a number."

"Three," I replied.

"One, two, three. Now pick another number."

"One," I said.

Mr. Burles lifted up the flap of the paper fortune teller that Anna made and read it aloud to me, "You will get to third base tonight—"

"Omigod," I said to myself, uncomfortable with the implication I was somehow going to go to third base with his daughter. When Anna crafted that prediction, she wasn't referring to me and her, it was just a silly thing she wrote on the flap.

"Okay, that's it, Danny, time to go! NOW!" Mr. Burles yelled in my direction.

I knew nothing I would say or do would matter in that moment because the origami said I was going to get to third base, and he took that as fact. I stood up and gathered my art supplies, stuffed them into my backpack, and got ready to head out the door as instructed.

"Danny's gay!" Anna yelled. "GAY," she repeated, sounding like Brittany Murphy in *Drop Dead Gorgeous*.

Like a bullet straight into my heart. It would be a whole decade until I would actually accept the terms and conditions of being homosexual myself, so I certainly wasn't prepared to be outed just so I could play M.A.S.H. in my classmate's bedroom.

I ran out of the room as fast as I could and hopped on my bike to ride home, horrified, crying the entire way, not because I was kicked out of my friend's house, but because maybe Anna was right. Facing the truth can be much harder than ignoring it. From then on, every single time I'd have feelings for another guy, I would do everything I could to stop them, remembering the tears that fell to the dirt road on my bike ride home from Anna's house. Even during my senior spring break when I snuck off to that gay bar and kissed my Myrtle Beach man, I hustled back to my hotel room and cried alone in the bathroom, those same middle school feelings flooding back to me. I worried that being gay meant I would never fall in love or have kids. I worried that everyone who did love me would stop if they knew I had been lying to them about it, even though I didn't exactly know who I was myself.

Those years when you're figuring it all out can be mental torture, but if you can get through them, you can have your moment in the rain, when all that self-loathing and confusion washes away, and you realize that life doesn't stop when you come out. In fact, life begins because you're finally living it authentically.

Once everyone knew I was gay, I stopped caring about what I liked or didn't like and how it was perceived by others. If I want to memorize the spoken word intro to Monica and Brandy's "The Boy Is Mine" song, I will. If I want to go to a solo matinee of the Little Women remake, I'll go. There are things that society still considers masculine or for boys, things like sports or cars, and then there are things like dresses and dolls that are still considered only appropriate for women. These labels can be so harmful, and it's time we rid ourselves of the stereotypes. Like what you like, and know that if it isn't harming others, it's okay. I know men who love to play with makeup, women who like football, and nonbinary people who like both. Some of those people are straight, some are gay, others bisexual, and many who identify as something else.

A family friend recently told me that his seven-year-old son wanted a Barbie, and he was afraid to buy it for him. He said if his son never has the doll, he won't know what he's missing, but it's the dad who is the one who is going to be missing something. He'll be missing who his son really is, and he'll be missing the tears that will be happening on those bike rides home.

FLAME GAME

M.A.S.H. is a classic, and I HIGHLY recommend that you partner up with a buddy to play, but in the meantime, FLAME is a game that can be played with a friend OR solo, so let's all take a moment to have some fun, shall we? For this example, we'll determine what your relationship with Idris Elba *should* be. You can substitute Idris Elba with any of your favorite leading men. I chose Idris because I just watched the movie *Molly's Game*, where he's looking flawless in a suit, and I honestly cannot stop thinking about it. If you're someone who is not into Idris Elba (seems impossible, but whatevs), substitute his name with someone to your liking, physically. It's a fantasy, so get creative. No judgment here.

INSTRUCTIONS:

☞ Write your name above Idris Elba.

Example:

Danny Pellegrino

Idris Elba

☞ Cross off the common letters. (Remove any letters that are shared by both names.) For this example, we are left with:

~~DA~~ N N Y ~~PELLE~~ G ~~RI~~ N O

~~IDRI~~ S ~~EL~~ B ~~A~~

☞ Count the remaining letters (the ones that haven't been crossed out). In this case, there are 8 because the only letters that aren't shared between the two names are the three N's, the Y, the G, and the O in my name and the S and the B in his name.

☞ Write down the word FLAME.

FLAME stands for Friendship, Love, Affection, Marriage, and Enemies.

☞ Count through the letters in the word FLAME, and when you land on the number of letters you had remaining, cross out that letter. In my case it was 8, so every time I am counting and get to 8, I cross out that letter. Begin counting again with the remaining letters. Continue until all but one letter in FLAME is crossed out. In my example, I'm left with the letter F.

☞ Whatever letter you are left with, that is the relationship you are destined to have with Idris Elba. In my case, sadly, I'm destined to just be *friends* with Idris. Looks like I'll have to play again using my legal name, Daniel Pellegrino, until I get what I want.

HERE IS YOUR LETTER GUIDE:

F = Friendship   A = Affection (sex)   E = Enemies

L = Love   M = Marriage

Butts & Kelly

I know I said I would change the names in this book, but it's imperative that in this next story I maintain the truth that is Butts and Kelly.
Butts and Kelly are two small, mixed-breed dogs that belonged to a
piano teacher I had—Miss Donna.

My parents were more of a sports family, rarely pushing me and
my brothers into the creative arts, but we did have family friends who
had a daughter my age and would often sign me up for things like
drawing class or piano lessons. I can't sing, but around middle school
I saw *Divas Live 1998* and figured if I can't sing like those queens did
during the "Natural Woman" finale, at least I could play an instrument
near the women who could. So Mom signed me up for weekly piano
lessons at Miss Donna's house, a quirky woman in her late sixties who
lived alone with Butts, Kelly, and a wide array of horse photos adorn-
ing her walls, which she would talk to as if they were in the room.

"My horsey!" she'd say in an adult baby voice that would send
chills down anyone's spine, pointing to a framed image above the
piano. The equestrian decor was all different, some were oil paintings,

others looked like they were drawn in the style of *Bob's Burgers*. The only through line was that there were horses featured in every hung piece. You know how some people have kitchens filled with word art from HomeGoods? It was like that, only instead of Live, Laugh, Love signs, there was horse art everywhere.

Detour

HomeGoods is my favorite place on earth. I'm never more at peace than when I'm walking the aisles, browsing the cooking oils, shuffling through the racks of towels, or rummaging the holiday merch section for seasonal gnomes. It's pure bliss, but it's *imperative* that you curate your shopping trip. We've all made mistakes there before, getting a little too excited after grabbing the cart, throwing everything that sparks joy inside of it. You ladies know what I'm talking about. Marie Kondo wants us to get rid of shit, but I can only assume that's because she's never been inside of a HomeGoods. Whenever I'm there, like Ashley Tisdale in *High School Musical 3*, I want it all. Regardless, you MUST look at your cart before you head to the checkout and remove some stuff. Count your word art and remove at least one item. There's a famous saying about removing an accessory before you leave the house, and I beseech you to remove one Rae Dunn original from your HomeGoods cart before you're even close enough for a cashier to say, "Who's next?" While I'm here offering tips, be sure to leave enough time in your shopping experience for those items near the register, which is where some of my favorite finds are. Plus, you should have extra room in your cart after giving up a find. I love the artisanal orange slices and creative s'more-type treats that you can't get anywhere else (except TJ Maxx, Marshalls, etc.). Don't let anyone rush you when you're looking through those candies and cards. Relax. Settle in. Let patrons go ahead of you if they are in a rush. Savor the moments near the register, and if you've curated the items properly, you can add a few extras from the checkout area to your cart before paying and leave the heavenly store with pride. These rules also apply to the aforementioned TJ Maxx, where I'm a certified Maxxinista, and Marshalls, which, together with HomeGoods, make up the triumvirate of Midwest shopping, all of which would be flawless experiences if it weren't for the hellish way they put price stickers on their items. Why must it be so hard to get the $12.99 tag off my candle? Whose idea was it to plaster it on the middle of my glass mirror? When will our elected officials take this on?!

The first time I went to Miss Donna's house, I was overwhelmed by the smell of urine, but I initially didn't quite know how to place the scent. *Hoarders* had not been on the air at that point, so I didn't have the language to describe exactly what I saw, but this woman had definitely collected way too many knickknacks and had very clearly never left her home. Kids would stop by after school, she would teach them hand placement on the keys, and then I can only assume Miss Donna would cuddle up with Butts and Kelly to watch *Dharma & Greg*.

When I would arrive at her house for my 4:30 p.m. lesson, Butts and Kelly would be sanctioned off in the kitchen, while Miss Donna's piano was a few feet away, ready to be played. There are yappy dogs, and then there's Butts and Kelly. They were *very* protective of Miss

Donna, so anytime anyone would arrive, they would bark like hell from the kitchen, and the woofs wouldn't stop for the entire hour. It felt loud, like *Man of Steel*–soundtrack loud. I'd be playing "Chopsticks" and Butts and Kelly would be barking along, off-key, just a few steps away from me.

I don't know what exactly Miss Donna should've done about Butts and Kelly. Perhaps she could've put them in another room or found some space outside for them to hang while she taught her students. Instead, she would spend the hour yelling at them while I tried to learn the notes. She would be so kind, gentle, and sweet with me but lost it on them.

"C-E-F-G..." she'd softly say in that adult baby voice as I played "When the Saints Go Marching In."

By the time I hit the G, Butts and Kelly would begin their bark.

"BUTTS! KELLY! SHUT UP!" she would shout in a deep baritone at them, going from zero to one hundred like the best Real Housewives do, only instead of a designer wrap dress, Miss Donna was wearing a T-shirt with Flicka on it.

"Should I keep playing?" I'd ask.

"Yes, hun, keep going, I'm listening."

C-E-F-G-

"Ruff!"

"BUTTS! KELLY! SHUT UP! I WILL HIT YOU WITH A TWO-BY-FOUR!" Miss Donna screamed.

"Is everything okay?" I queried.

"Hun, yes, of course, just keep playing."

"Ruff! Ruff!!"

"HEY, BUTTS! HEY, KELLY! SHUT UP! IF YOU DON'T, I WILL GET THE TWO-BY-FOUR! You know who doesn't bark? HORSES DON'T BARK!"

This continued for exactly one hour, every single lesson. Each week. Pure chaos. For what it's worth, I never saw any physical abuse, and I truly don't think she had a two-by-four handy, but she did continue to threaten them.

After the second lesson, I talked to my friend who also had classes with Miss Donna.

"Does she yell at Butts and Kelly while you're in there too?"

"Yeah, she tells them she is going to hit them with a two-by-four," my friend replied.

"Have you ever seen her do it? Like, does she have wood?"

"I don't think so."

"Isn't it distracting? I can never get through one song because she has to keep stopping and starting," I admitted.

"Yeah, but my mom says she offers the cheapest lessons in town."

Turns out we were getting budget lessons. We could've gone to the local music school and paid an arm and a leg to take professional classes from an expert, but we decided to drive over to Miss Donna's house once a week and get the knockoff version, complete with an out-of-tune piano and the aggressive relationship she had with her two dogs.

Miss Donna never planned on using lumber. She used to live on a farm and moved to the suburbs, where there was no space for horses, and she figured dogs were the next best thing. Butts and Kelly barked because they knew they would never live up to the horses Miss Donna held so dear. Every day those cute pooches had to look around the room and see endless horse paraphernalia, knowing that they would never be the animals that Miss Donna wanted them to be. Sometimes when I'm on Instagram, looking at my feed, which is filled with hot male models, I think about Butts and Kelly. Those dogs were constantly faced with the image of the ones they would not live up to. And Miss Donna was frustrated because the life she built for herself didn't allow her to spend time with the creatures she really loved.

After less than a year of not learning anything at the lessons with Miss Donna, my mom stopped taking me. I can only play one song ("When the Saints Go Marching In") on the piano, but I did learn some valuable lessons: You get what you pay for, and life is a compromise. Oh, and horses don't bark.

No

"Look alive!"

DAD, EVERY TIME I WALKED ONTO A FIELD/COURT TO PLAY A
SPORT I WASN'T INTERESTED IN AS A CHILD.

Somewhere around 2010, the idea of saying yes to everything became a popular mantra. Agreeing to anything that is offered to you in a literal sense was encouraged, but if there's one thing I've learned from reading Amelia Bedelia and watching Kathy Hilton on *The Real Housewives of Beverly Hills*, it's that not everything is meant to be taken literally. If someone asks you to draw the curtains, you don't need a sketch pad, and if someone asks you to do something you're not into, you don't need to say yes, despite what self-help books and improv teachers tell you. As someone who has spent thousands of dollars and the entirety of his twenties taking improv classes, I can confidently say that the rules of improvisation are not always to be taken as fact or practiced in your everyday life.

Sure, getting out of your comfort zone can be a good thing. I never loved seafood as a kid, but eventually, as an adult, I tried a piece of sushi and I LIKED IT. If I hadn't gotten outside of my comfort zone, I never would've discovered that my taste buds were turned on by a California roll (to be honest, my love of sushi is limited to basically just a California roll, so perhaps I should've used a better example here). The point is, it can be a good thing, but not *always*. Sometimes you need to say no, whether for your own sanity or for the sake of your kids' well-being.

A lot of the yes or no decisions are made for you as a child. Most of my peers played soccer when I was growing up, and I was certainly no exception thanks to my parents' decision-making. Little league sports are a rite of passage in northeast Ohio, and the older you get, the more you start to pick and choose what extracurriculars you're into and discover what you're good at. But those early days were about playing it all and my parents saying yes.

My dad wasn't an absent father, but he worked. A lot. Usually he was dragging me and my brothers along to help out at the factory where he spent his days, teaching us wonderful life lessons about work ethic and the value of a dollar. School taught us money basics via selling magazine subscriptions and earning currency in the form of colorful pompom creatures called "weepuls," but everything else we needed to learn at home. Mom was employed too, but she was part-time and otherwise home making sure the house was in order and food was on the table. Because of all this, Dad would sometimes miss dinners or school plays or sports games. I was recently watching *Jingle All the Way*, an unhinged Christmas film that was seemingly written for Tim Allen or Martin Lawrence but was instead led by Arnold

Schwarzenegger as Howard, a hardworking father who occasionally misses his son's activities, and he's looked at as a monster by the other characters for doing so. The older I get, the more I appreciate how hard my dad busted his ass and how he and Howard didn't deserve the holiday pressure that was placed on them by society, the kid from *Star Wars,* and Rita Wilson. There's this narrative that a working family man (or woman) is bad, but I see them as doing what's necessary to build a better life for their kids, and although my dad might've missed an event or two, he did his best and showed us how hard you have to hustle to get ahead in life. His incredible work ethic taught me that any dream I had was possible, but that I would have to make sacrifices to achieve it, and I'm forever grateful.

Mom, on the other hand, wasn't always thrilled with his hours, and she would encourage him to take time off when he could to coach our little league teams or help out in our other extracurriculars. This culminated in him coaching my soccer team in the fifth grade, a sport he didn't even know the rules to and has never once played himself.

Back in the '90s, kids' sports were a bit different than I imagine they are now. I can vividly remember baseball games where the dads would drink Miller Lite while they watched, and then they would get into verbal and physical fights with the young volunteer referees/umpires. It wasn't unusual for a dad nicknamed Big Billy to get in the face of a local umpire at a baseball game for twelve-year-olds. Big Billy would verbally abuse a sixteen-year-old for miscounting the outs, and most of the other neighborhood dads were engaging in similar activities. I've heard grown men call teenage umps "rat bastards" through a cloud of beer breath at 2:00 p.m. on a Saturday, and no one on the sidelines batted an eyelash. It was as if the behavior was as commonplace as handing out Capri Suns after the game. There were also plenty of dads smoking cigarettes *while* coaching first base. IT WAS THE ERA.

Anyway, Dad decided one year to take on my soccer team, and it was a hot mess. We didn't win a single game, and every kid left that season as a worse player. Somehow everyone regressed in talent. The pinnacle of the year was when he thought it would be a good idea to attempt a "flying V" like they did in the Mighty Ducks movies. I was OBSESSED with the Mighty Ducks movies, and my pops knew that. If you're not familiar, it's a Disney movie trilogy about a hockey team who sucks but then gets good when Coach Gordon Bombay takes over. It's Gordon's punishment for drunk driving, which…what the F was that about? Anyway, he teaches the kids a play called the *flying V*, where the offense skates in a V shape, passing the hockey puck around to each other on the ice before scoring. It worked in the film because of movie magic, but I think even filmmakers assumed that everyone would see it as a haphazard play that wouldn't be successful in real life, and never once did they assume anyone would try to do this play AT A KID'S SOCCER GAME.

We spent a whole practice trying to do it, never once perfecting it or even coming close to doing it in an acceptable way. Even so, when game day came along and our team was down by four, Dad huddled everyone during a time out and gave us a rousing speech that would leave Al Pacino in *Any Given Sunday* shook.

"The biggest battle of our professional lives comes down to today. We're in hell right now, gentlemen. We can stay here and lose, or we can fight our way out of the hell. I think back on my youth—" he began.

"Dad, this isn't halftime, they're going to start playing without us," I interrupted.

"Let's do the flying V! Now let's caw!" he instructed.

What the fuck's a caw? I thought.

"You mean a quack?" I asked.

"Yeah, whatever the hell they did in that movie, I never watched it," Dad replied before our team began to let out a few stray quacks.

The referee blew his whistle, and with control of the ball, five pre-pubescent boys with zero soccer talent got into a V shape, only to quickly lose authority of it. We went from what could only be described as a cursive F shape to the opposing team scoring on us yet again. We lost the game by seven.

Our team never attempted any fancy moves again, and Dad never offered his services to the sport of soccer. He has many, many skills, but that was not one of them. He said yes when he wasn't qualified and also probably didn't even want to do it. While self-help books may say otherwise, I'm here to encourage you all to occasionally come from a place of no.

The RetURN

You'll notice I talk a lot about grief because it is still one of those topics people do their best to sideswipe. I'm not even sure why it's so taboo. Someone you've loved for years, who was a constant in your life, suddenly (or even worse, slowly) passes away, and you're supposed to continue on living your life, working your day job, and acting like the person people expect you to be all the while dealing with an intense inner turmoil that is low-key telling you to hide under the covers and cry.

The first time I experienced true grief was in middle school when my dog died. I can feel some of you rolling your eyes reading this, but it was very traumatic and my first grasp of the idea that lives come to an end. Up until then, I had some distant relatives pass, but no one close to me. My dog dying was like starter grief. Her name was Cuddles, a silly title even for a dog, and she was an adorable cocker spaniel–poodle mix, who never left my mom's side. When Cuddles was around twelve years old, she started to get sick. The first trip to the vet resulted in some expensive medication that made her feel better, but pretty soon those meds weren't enough. I still don't know exactly what was wrong with her. My parents kept it hidden, perhaps because it was too hard to talk about, or maybe I just didn't ask enough questions as an angsty fourteen year old.

One Friday night, my school hosted an all-night charity event at the football field. People from all over town stayed the night in tents and raised money for cancer research, and when I left for the event on Friday night, everything was fine. The next morning, I caught a ride home around 6:00 a.m. and I went straight to bed, exhausted from staying up all night with my buddies.

By afternoon, some of my friends who lived in the neighborhood came by the house to hang out. One of them was a girl named Brenda, who, back then, I thought was the love of my life. As you'll learn from other chapters of this book, she was one of many. Young love becomes an obsession at times. You imagine your future with that person, and a little smile from them is enough to sustain the longing for months on end until the feelings subside, and you move on to someone else. For a brief moment in time, Brenda was *the one*. At least she was until Sarah. And then Tina. And eventually Ryan. Anyway, Brenda was beautiful, yes, but also she had a quick wit and a biting personality. By biting per-sonality, I mean she was an asshole, but no one called her on it because she was meaner than everyone else and so the entire school wanted her approval. I'm not sure if I was so much in love with her as I was in desperate need of that approval. Either way, I spent many days that spring listening to "How Do I Live" by LeAnn Rimes on repeat and daydreaming about a life with Brenda, while also hoping she wouldn't call me gay in front of everyone like she so often would. All of this was, of course, a precursor to my days spent listening to Brandy's "Have You Ever" on repeat...ah, youth.

I woke up that afternoon to the sound of the doorbell ringing, suddenly remembering I had made plans to ride bikes with the group, but really I just wanted to see Brenda. When I got out of my room, my mom was welcoming my friends into the house like she always does, only this time she had her glasses on instead of the usual contact lenses she would wear. Anytime she had the glasses on during the day, I knew something was wrong because it was likely she was crying. Tears aren't conducive to contacts. In the five hours I had been catching up on my sleep, my dog Cuddles had passed away. My mom had spent those hours bawling her eyes out and waiting for me to wake up so she could deliver the news, surely not expecting that time to coincide my dream girl slash bully coming by.

"What's going on?" I asked my mom.

"Sweetie, I'm so sorry, Cuddles—"

She couldn't even finish the sentence. The tears started flowing and she was sobbing. I knew. Overwhelmed with emotion, I started to well up too, only I was afraid of showing too much emotion in front of my crush. Liquid hadn't even left my eyes when I noticed Brenda and the others started laughing at our sadness. Mom quickly excused herself to the other room. I'm not even entirely certain she saw them chuckling or if she just wanted to pull herself together for me.

I felt like I had been hit by a bus. Not only was I running on five hours of sleep in two days, but I was finding out that my dog died in front of an audience. Kids are cruel, and we all handle awkward moments differently, but this was especially tough for all involved.

They had come by the house to invite me outside to ride bikes or play a game, and instead they were smack-dab in the middle of Pellegrino family grief. Although I understood the reaction, their nervous laughter felt cruel, and instead of telling them to get the hell out of the house, I pushed my tears down and suggested we go outside. Anything to get out of the house of sadness.

We played in the open air until early evening, and anytime I thought about my dog or the puddle of tears I left my mom in, I did my best to push those emotions away and keep my eyes dry. I was actively ignoring the grief, horrified by what Brenda was thinking of me with every passing moment. Through the corner of my eye, I'd spot her whispering to another kid, giggling about my sadness. I'd continue yearning for her approval for a couple more years, but that was the day I realized Brenda was not the love of my life.

Over the next couple of decades, I found new loves and experienced more grief. Although I love the holidays, it can be an especially sad time and also a time when we think about all those in our lives who are no longer with us, whether it be the dogs or people we've lost along the way, but this isn't a story about my loss...

Detour

Speaking of Christmas and sadness, who among us hasn't related deeply to the woman covered in birds in *Home Alone 2*? She's unspeakably lonely...literally barely talking throughout the entire film despite being the female lead. Eventually she does open up to Kevin McCallister, only for him to ditch her completely after they become besties and she saves his life from the robbers using her bird power.

On Christmas morn, after Kevin's family arrives in New York City and they wake up in the Plaza Hotel with a room full of gifts from Mr. Duncan, Kevin runs off to see his fowl friend. Rather than invite her in for a meal and a shower to wash the pigeon shit off her cold body, Kevin simply brings her an ORNAMENT. What the hell is she going to do with an ornament? She doesn't have a house! I suppose she could hang it on one of the trees in Central Park every year, but quite (uncle) frankly, I think she would've preferred to be invited inside for some holiday cheer. It all just proves that Linnie McCallister was right in the first film; Kevin is what the French call "les incompetents."

Christmas can be even more challenging when the loss is fresh. Years after Cuddles, I came home for Christmas with my boyfriend. My immediate family has expanded quite a bit now that I'm an adult. Both my brothers have wives and kids, and those wives have their own brothers and sisters and parents. And because of all my nieces and nephews, I typically order gifts online and have them shipped to my parents' house, where I stay when I'm in Ohio. Inevitably, when I get into town and survey all the items I ordered as gifts while drunk at home watching the Hallmark Channel's Countdown to Christmas, there are items that need to be returned. Sometimes I see that I ordered the wrong size or a duplicate arrives. It's a hassle, but I try to get everything sorted as soon as possible, since I'm only home for a few days.

One year I got to town and noticed that three of my items needed to be sent back to Amazon. Luckily, in northeast Ohio there is an Amazon drop-off center in the back of a Kohl's store. If you've never been to Kohl's, know that it's a magical place where you can buy just about everything, like ten different types of K-Cup organizers alongside sexy underwear, gourmet chocolates, and old Wii games.

"Can I borrow the car? I need to return some stuff," I asked my mom.

"There's a box in the front seat with a couple things I've been meaning to send back to Amazon too. Can you take those in for me?" she replied.

"Sure."

"And I'm gonna give you some money to pick up Elsa pajamas for Sophia, give me a minute," she said as she went for her purse in the other room.

I'm not made of money, but I certainly can afford to front the cash for a pair of *Frozen* pajamas for my mom to give my niece. Little did I know that my mom didn't go treasure hunting for singles when she excused herself—she was looking for the thing that all mothers have in an old envelope that is bursting at the seams...Kohl's Cash. For my brother's bachelor party, we went to a strip club. As one of two best men, I made sure to stop by an ATM to get a plentiful stack of singles to give the dancers. I got us a stack of a hundred ones to make it rain, and that stack paled in comparison to the width of my mom's handful of Kohl's Cash.

"Use this," she said, handing me her most prized possession.

Eyes wide, I fanned the retail papers and pulled one out to examine it up close.

"Don't worry about the expiration date, Dan. The cashiers let you use it even after it expires," Mom said assuredly.

I gathered up my items, tossed them in the passenger seat, and headed off to the store on Christmas Eve with the thick envelope in my pocket. Kohl's on Christmas Eve is intense with an electric energy. Stores in general on Christmas Eve are usually filled with angry patrons, but for some reason, Kohl's bucks that holiday trend and everyone is happy, albeit rushed.

Parking was a challenge, but I eventually found a spot only a mile away from the double-door entrance. Exhausted, I carried my boxes, along with my mom's items to the store, and once inside, I knew I had to walk all the way to the back to find the Amazon drop-off center. It would be too easy for them to place the return booth in the front, and to be honest, it's a brilliant business move. Customers will inevitably find a million items on their way to return just a few. If my hands were free, I would've picked up a travel pillow, Minion slippers, and a beer Koozie that said, *Beer Me, Daddy.*

When I arrived at the Amazon kiosk and greeted the exhausted employee who was ready to take my goods, I surveyed my haul to make sure I had everything. Mom's box had two items, a Fisher-Price toy that she mistakenly purchased and what seemed to be a vase. I handed the employee my items and looked at the return receipt my mom had in her box. There was only one item marked on the slip to be sent back. I figured I should unwrap the vase to take a closer look in case it went with the Fisher-Price. Turns out it wasn't, in fact, a vase. It was an urn, like where they put dead people.

A relative had passed a few days prior and my parents were involved in the services, but I didn't realize they bought the container that holds the remains, from an online retailer no less. The employee could see me mentally putting the pieces together, and the look of sheer terror that suddenly took over my face is something she will likely never forget.

"Did I just bring my dead relative into a Kohl's on Christmas Eve to run some returns?" I silently worried.

Cautiously, I shook the urn, saying a silent prayer to Mariah Carey that there weren't any ashes in my arms. The emptiness was a relief, and my butthole was able to de-clench for a few brief moments. Although there was no one in it, I still didn't know if I was supposed to return it with the other Amazon products, so I called my mom to get some intel.

"Why would you return an urn to Kohl's?" she asked me over the phone, saying it as if I were crazy for bringing an urn into a Kohl's, and somehow it was perfectly normal for her to have an empty urn from an online retailer in the front seat of her car alongside a preschool toy.

"It was in the box!" I told her.

"Don't return it! We need it. And don't forget to get the Elsa pajamas!" she instructed before hanging up the phone in a holiday hurry.

My butthole clenched again knowing that I would have to shop through the busy aisles holding an urn in one hand and my Kohl's

Cash in the other on one of the biggest shopping days of the year. To make matters worse, browsing the children's clothing section always makes me uncomfortable. The pajamas are near the kid underwear, and no decent grown man wants to be in the little girl's underwear section, with or without an urn.

I quickly raced through the aisles, grabbed the first pair of pajamas I saw with Tony award-winner Idina Menzel's character on them and hurried to the line. There are lines in hell that are shorter than the Kohl's holiday line. It wrapped around the entire store. I found the end, and I waited behind an older gal who was solo and in front of a young teenage couple ho-ho-hoeing with some aggressive PDA. It's nice to see people in love, but no one should be so in love that they are tongue-kissing in a department store line on Jesus's birthday. Enough.

Kohl's at Christmas is also like a fucking high school reunion, so that meant I was running into everyone I know. First an old English teacher, Ms. Denise, came up to say hello.

"Danny Pellegrino! I haven't seen you in years!" she said.

"Hi. Merry Christmas," I promptly replied, hoping she would take the hint and keep walking.

"What do you got there? Gifts?" she asked, looking straight at the urn.

"No, it's an urn. See ya later!"

Ms. Denise looked at me sideways and continued on her shopping trip with just the slightest whiplash, while the woman in front of me looked back with a scrunched nose and judgy eyes, like I was poisonous. It wasn't until after Ms. Denise was gone that I realized my lack of sharing details made it seem like I *did* actually have the remains of someone along with me on my shopping trip.

My voice must've carried because suddenly I heard, "Danny, is that you?" from a few spots ahead in line. It was coming from Brenda (BRENDA!), the girl I thought I loved in middle school. I hadn't seen her for years, maybe even a decade, and she had clearly been waiting in line even longer than me, so she wasn't about to give up her spot to walk closer to me. Instead, she decided to have a conversation with me through the other customers.

"Why do you have an urn?!" she shouted from afar.

"No one's in it! Nobody, or no bodies, I should say!" I told her loudly, overcompensating for moments prior. I felt like I was transported right back into my young teen years, desperate for this person's approval once again. It had been years since I had a romantic crush on her, and I wasn't even interested in having a relationship with her gender at this point in my life, but alas, I fell back into that pattern of behavior. To prove that the container was empty, I lifted the top and shook the urn upside down to show that there were no ashes inside, unfortunately not realizing that there was something inside: a small piece of paper with instructions on it. I'm still not certain what kind of instructions you need with an urn. Don't you just put the ashes in it? Regardless, the manual floated like the Hope in *Hope Floats*, and I was afraid to leave my spot to get it. Instead, I just let it drift and offered up a joke to my audience about what flew out of the urn...

"That's no one! Unless they recycled my cousin into a sheet of paper!"

Like one of the many improv shows I put on throughout my twenties for tens of people, there were no laughs from the majority of the crowd. Brenda did, however, start to smile at me in that devious and familiar way, as if she was making fun of me in her head, preparing what she would tell her friends about our run-in, laughing at me over a box of wine. She turned back around to face the registers, and that was the end of our conversation, with her eventually waving goodbye after she finished checking out. Meanwhile, the woman in front of me picked up the urn instructions and handed them to me.

By the time I reached the register, I just wanted the holiday season to be over so I could return to my cocoon and forget about the gifts and the embarrassment. Defeated, I handed the cashier my Kohl's Cash for the Disney pajamas.

"I heard you talking about that," the checkout woman said, pointing to the urn in my arms.

"Mm-hmm," I responded.

"You're not the first person who shops with one of those," the cashier said, "There's a man who brings his wife's remains in here every Sunday. He says it was her favorite place to shop."

I was so worried that the town would think I was shopping with someone's ashes that I didn't even stop to think about what would be so wrong if I was. We all handle grief differently, and there's no right or wrong way to go about saying goodbye or keeping someone with you. We're all just doing the best we can. Whether you're chugging a box of wine to cope, taking six-hour midday naps, setting up Christmas decorations in May, robbing a bank, or giving yourself bangs, you're doing what you need to do to survive, and that's okay with me. Some of us are taking our loved ones with us metaphorically, while others are taking them to their favorite stores inside of an urn.

Judging Judy

It's hard for me to watch a movie and let it go, particularly when I love it. I'm the type of person who will hop on IMDB immediately after the credits roll to check out the trivia section, find out what other movies the fifth lead has appeared in, and download the soundtrack on Spotify. I become obsessed. Never was this more so than after I saw the movie *Judy*, starring Renée Zellweger. I felt invigorated after, as if I were in a coma and I finally came to! By the way, if any of you ever need to actually wake me up from a coma, put headphones on my ears and play the last forty-five seconds of any Christina Aguilera song. I'll wake up.

Renée plays the legendary Judy Garland in the biopic, which follows her life story, specifically focusing on the later years. I've always loved the music icon, who was actually born Frances Ethel Gumm, but things escalated after the 2019 film. I listened to "The Trolley Song" on repeat and began reading every book I could find about her and anyone related to her. This kind of behavior is fine if you're alone, but when you're in a relationship, it can be a lot for the significant other to take in.

My boyfriend has different interests than I do, and I think that's why our relationship works. He's into gritty murder mysteries, while I prefer a movie with a diva, directed by Nancy Meyers, and/or starring one of the Hunts (Bonnie Hunt, Helen Hunt, or Holly Hunter). When I dragged him to see *Judy*, he was checking his watch the whole time while I breathed it all in, enamored with every frame of cinema in front of me. For weeks after, I would blast "Get Happy" or "Come Rain or Come Shine" when I got in the shower or cooked dinner. There was nary a minute inside our apartment when Judy wasn't singing through one of the speakers. Siri, Google, Alexa, and all the other robot people in our home got to know Ms. Garland. When "Over the Rainbow" or one of her other songs wasn't playing, I was humming it. Eventually, he grew tired, and things came to a head on a particular Saturday.

We made plans to see some friends in the park for a picnic in the early afternoon, but we couldn't stay long for because we had an early work dinner thing with his boss. I was in *Judy* mode at lunch, so I brought up the movie and performance to anyone who would listen.

"Did you see *Judy*?"

"Wasn't Renée excellent?"

"I loved the music."

"I was surprised how perfectly she captured her essence."

"'The Trolley Song' has always been amazing, but I have a new appreciation for it."

"I love the part where she sings about the clang, clang."

"I think she's going to win another Oscar."

My boyfriend rolled his eyes throughout the entire soiree. Being in a relationship with me is exhausting, and he was past the point of embarrassment. When we got in the car to head home, he told me I had a problem. It was an intervention.

"It's just so good, how is anyone not talking about how good it is?" I said to him in the car.

"Literally talk about anything else! Pick another movie or TV show or subject. Anything!" he pleaded.

"You're being dramatic," I said.

"Dramatic? That word is familiar because you used it a hundred times at the park talking about how Renée nailed the drama of Judy without going over the top with her performance!" he yelled.

"Okay, so maybe I bring it up once in a while, but it's topical!" I said.

"She died in the 1960s!"

"BUT THE MOVIE JUST CAME OUT!"

Our war of words was escalating, and I knew I had to diffuse it.

"I don't HAVE to talk about it."

"I bet you can't go the rest of the day without bringing it up," he threatened.

"Come on! Of course I can. It's not like I'm going to bring it up to your boss at dinner. I don't even know your boss."

"He's a straight man, and there's no straight man that is going to want to hear you talk about Judy Garland for an entire dinner," he said.

"Fine! I promise no Judy. And if I do mention her, I'll make dinner every night for a month."

"Deal."

"DEAL!"

When we arrived at home, I showered without the soundtrack

playing, knowing that I needed to cleanse not just the dirt from the outdoor picnic, but the sounds of Liza's mother from my brain. The songs were already stuck in my head, and I didn't need the refresher right before dinner.

Our meal was at a nice restaurant with not just my boyfriend's boss, but the boss's wife, another gay couple that works at the company, and a stray, single woman I believe was related to the boss and in town visiting, but who was never properly introduced to any of us. She just sat down, and the boss told us that she was shy and sad because her girlfriend just broke up with her, so that's all we knew about this extra person at the table. Everyone was too afraid to ask her any questions because of her fragile state, and no one really wanted to be there anyway. This was one of those dinners you're forced to do a few times a year when you would rather pack your knives and go home to watch *Top Chef*.

On the way to dinner, I was reminded of our bet, and I assured my boyfriend that I would not only refrain from bringing up the movie, I also wouldn't talk about anything that Renée was ever in. That meant no *Bridget Jones*, *Jerry Maguire*, or even *Cold Mountain*, a film with the most deranged accent work in the history of cinema from not only Renée but Nicole Kidman and Jude Law. They're all talking from a different region and it's beautiful to watch unfold. Renée removes the letters from the end of almost every word she speaks in *Cold Mountain*, so she says dialog like, "I ain' servin', if ya get my meanin'," or "I ain' neve' care fo' nothin', I ain' lookin' fo' money, I ain' wort nothin'," all the while her body moves in such a youthful way, she's like a real life version of Angelica Pickles from *Rugrats* who wants to kill chickens with her bare hands and never learned the letter "g."

"If they bring the movie *Judy* up, I *can* talk about it though, right?" I asked my boyfriend.

"Fine, but they're not going to bring up the movie."

"You don't know that!" I said.

We arrived at the overpriced steakhouse around the same time as the others, and shortly after we greeted everyone and sat down, we were already out of things to talk about. I find that fancy dinners are awkward, even if you're close with all of the guests. There's something about the uncomfortability of multiple forks that makes everyone a little less themselves. I'm normally able to break the ice and be as chatty as needed, but I was so scared to say just about anything, realizing that without *Judy*, I didn't have much of a personality. Perhaps I had become too obsessed.

Things started to get super quiet post apps. We already ran through the standard "how are you" and "where are you from" pleasantries before the entrées, and no one else seemed eager to spark any other dialogue. As much as I love my boyfriend, he's not the type to bring up new topics at the dinner table. He's one of those people who is completely comfortable in the silence, something I am not. I find there is always going to be conversation going on in my life, but if it's not happening with the people I'm with, then the discussion is going to be going on internally, which is certainly not something I need more of. I'm sick of the voices in my head.

The boss's wife was the slowest to finish her meal, cutting her pork chop into painstakingly small pieces. Everyone clearly wanted to wrap up the dinner, but she was keeping us there all night. I began to wonder if she just didn't want to have to go home with her husband and spend any more time alone with him. He initially seemed like he had the personality of a jar of mayonnaise, so part of me got it. The lesbian at one point asked the married woman bluntly, "Can you speed up?" One of the other gay men at the table laughed at the audacious comment, but she didn't say it as a joke. She wanted to get the hell out of there.

We all assumed we would wrap things up when the boss's wife was done, but before her plate was cleaned, the boss asked for the dessert menu. When he did, the bold lesbian sighed loudly on behalf of all of us.

"I need to bring up *Judy*; it's the only way to save this awkwardness," I thought to myself. The restriction was especially hard when our server asked, "You wantin' any dessert?" leaving off the *g* and making me think of Renée in *Cold Mountain*. As the thought passed through my mind, my boyfriend looked at me with intense eye contact. He knew what I was thinkin' and squashed it immediately. Knowin' that I couldn't bring it up, I decided to focus on findin' a way to get someone else to bring it up. After all, *Judy* was a semi-hit movie and Renée's performance was critically acclaimed. It was in the zeitgeist!

The most logical way for me to get someone else to bring up the movie was by mentioning my high school friend Judith, Jude for short. She never went by Judy, and instead of beautiful gowns and being in relationships with high-profile men, she spent four years as a virgin, wearing an aggressive amount of denim, but I figured hearing the name might spark something in one of the other dinner patrons.

"My friend Judith from high school is the best; she lives in San Francisco now. She takes those trolleys everywhere," I said, hoping *Judith* and *trolley* would ignite something. It didn't.

Not only did no one bite, but one of the gay men brought up *Fuller House*. FULLER HOUSE! Apparently the idea of San Francisco made him think of the Tanner family, which I actually completely get, but I was behind on my episodes at the time, so I DEFINITELY didn't want to talk about that show and have story lines ruined for me.

"My friend *Jude* lives near the house in that show. *Jude* loves the city, in rain or shine," I said, dropping as many hints as I could think of. Nothing.

"Jude, like that Beatles song," the boss said.

I understand that the Beatles are legends, but they aren't for me. I'd rather have all the *Fuller House* seasons spoiled than have to talk about the Beatles over dinner. Quite frankly, Kimmy Gibbler has had a greater impact on my world than Sir Paul, but that's beside the point.

"Shoot, I have to go feed the meter," my boyfriend said, looking at his watch, realizing how much time we had spent at this godforsaken restaurant.

He got up to leave the table, but before he did, he shot me another look. When you've been in a relationship for a long time, you can talk to each other without actually saying anything. A look says it all, and his said, "You better not fucking bring up that movie while I'm gone."

Without him monitoring me, I knew I could drop more aggressive hints to the rest of the group. I quickly mapped out where we parked and figured that I had approximately two minutes and forty-five seconds until my boyfriend would be back at the table. As soon as I spotted him out of the restaurant, I grabbed the dessert menu and began to hum "The Trolley Song."

"What's that song?" the wife asked.

"What song?" I replied.

"Never mind, must've been hearing things."

I hummed a little louder.

"I swear I know that song," one of the men said. At this point I was hoping that someone would pull out their phone and Shazam my vocals, but no one had the foresight.

Screw it, I thought. My guy was gone, and I was over this whole experience. I began to sing the clang portion of the chorus in that Judy way. Not only was I giving them lyrics, but I also did a little choreography, miming a top hat on my head and pretending to tip it to the rest of the dinner table.

Ordinarily, everyone around me would've chimed in, singing along to one of the most popular Judy Garland songs of all time. Instead, they all looked at me as if they saw a ghost. Although I didn't have a lot of preparation for my makeshift production, I certainly didn't think it was bad. What I didn't know is that my boyfriend was standing right behind me giving me another look. This time his look said, "Why are you the way that you are?"

I turned my head in shame. I couldn't even make it one dinner without bringing up the Judy Garland movie.

"I'm sorry."

"I forgot my wallet at home. Can I borrow some money for the meter?" he asked me.

"Sure," I replied as I handed over my wallet with deep regret. I would've given him my entire savings account if it meant I could erase my embarrassment.

"That's where I know that song! My mom used to call it 'The

Meter Song,'" the boss said. "Did you guys see the Judy movie? Renée was a revelation!" the only straight man at the table continued.

"We saw it last night, and he can't stop talking about it!" his wife added.

I lost the bet, so I spent the next month making all the dinners at home, but it was worth it. Not only did I spend twenty minutes talking about Renée over dessert that night, but my boyfriend's boss eventually gave him a promotion, one that I attribute to our shared love of *Judy*. When the Oscars finally came around and Ms. Zellweger won the trophy for best actress, I texted his boss.

"Our gal did it!" I exclaimed.

"She was the only dame for the job!" he said in that old Hollywood way.

Renée's acceptance speech included references to iconic figures like Venus and Serena, Selena, Bob Dylan, Martin Scorsese, and Fred Rogers, among others. It was a little rambling, but it was also beautiful because everyone at home watching the awards with new groups of friends could latch on to one of the legends that she mentioned. She surely sparked lots of conversation that evening, because pop culture is the great unifier. We all have different reference points, but if you can find the common ground, relationships can soar!

The Slow and the Furious

Vacation: Day Two

There are two types of vacationers—the tourists and the relaxers. If you're a tourist, you fill your entire schedule with excursions and activities, leaving almost no time to chill and (re)read Jessica Simpson's memoir in your hotel room while *NSYNC softly plays on your head-phones. The relaxers don't plan a single thing and instead spend their *entire* trip inside four walls or by a pool with a mojito. Activities exhaust me, but at the same time, I'm too anxious to spend too many days doing nothing, so I'm never very good at vacations. I don't fit in with either group, so I always tend to be doing something I don't want to do.

Detour

Speaking of *NSYNC, I live for a boy band, specifically the late '90s variety. The choreographed arm-ography, the vest work, the way one of them would always date one of the pop queens...if it weren't for the lingering threat of Y2K, it would've been a perfect time to be alive.

Even though I pledge my allegiance to the United States of Jessica Simpson, 98 Degrees was my early favorite of the boy bands of the era, which is surprising because they were...less than popular compared to *NSYNC and BSB. They were a boy band who often found themselves in that number three slot, while the others duked it out for the top. I always found myself rooting for 98 Degrees because they had the beefier guys, led by Jeff Timmons and Nick Lachey (from this point forward, I will be using asterisks for N*ck Lach*y as I want to show my support for my queen, Jessica Simpson). I liked that 98 Degrees seemed more like men instead of boys, which of course wasn't true, but to twelve-year-old me, it was. They were also the most mysterious, mostly because they got less press, and although Jeff was my clear favorite, I appreciated that three out of the four members would frequently appear without a blouse on national TV. While we're here, I did feel bad for the other one in the group, not Drew, the other, other one, who never took his top off and always had to wear a hat because if he didn't, he looked like a fifty-seven-year-old Realtor from North Carolina. I suppose I could Google his name right now, but his role was always to fade into the background, and so I will continue to honor that tradition here.

*NSYNC felt the most youthful of the three, although Joey Fatone was possibly in his late forties in 2000 and Chris Kirkpatrick's aggressive and ever-changing hair stylings and accessorizing made it unclear what year or planet he was born on. Mr. Kirkpatrick was always the focus of my "what the fuck is that," even when Chris was standing next to Joey during Joey's spiky red hair journey. Those two were both fronted by my king, JC Chasez, the second most important

JC after Jesus Christ. It's a close second because Jesus didn't have the cheekbones, turtleneck collection, or flawless vocals that Mr. Chasez had, but that's neither here nor there. I know their ramen-haired co-lead is off doing solo stuff, but I wish the group would do a reunion album and tour without him. JC could easily carry the vocals, and if they wanted another singer, they could enlist the help of their "Music of My Heart" partner, Gloria Estefan. As a bonus, audiences would get to hear "Turn the Beat Around" in between "Bye Bye Bye" and "This I Promise You." If Glo isn't interested, the group also did a duet with Rosie O'Donnell for her Christmas album, so that's an option too. Either works for me.

Song-wise, I think Backstreet Boys had the best bops, and it's important to note that Boyz II Men were the '90s blueprint for all the singing men, but let's all just take a moment of silence to appreciate all of the groups, shall we?

Where were we? Right, the infamous Florida vacation from my childhood. Growing up, my family didn't have a bunch of money to spend on trips; I didn't even ride on an airplane until I was in my late teens. We were blessed in plenty of other ways, but we balled on a budget for the early part of my life. Whenever we would travel, we would get to the hotel and immediately collect those pamphlets they usually have lining one of the walls in the lobby. You know the ones that give you information on magic shows, dinner theater, and the nearest slot machines? We would grab one of each and take them to our room to figure out the game plan for the remainder of the trip. As

I got older, the only thing I wanted on a family vacation was a henna tattoo and a pukka shell necklace, but in my preteen years, I was happy to help coordinate other activities. I started my life as a tourist type of vacationer. Usually those advertisements had coupons attached, and if they didn't, they got thrown in the trash. My parents had five mouths to feed, so we needed every discount we could gather.

Coupons aren't the only way to save money on a vacation, particularly in Florida. That's right, Orlando is home of the magical time-share tour. For the unfamiliar, a time-share tour is a simple 90-to-120-minute presentation of a vacation property that rewards participants with things like free tickets to theme parks and dinner vouchers for local buffets. The idea is that you'll buy a time-share after being sold on all the features in person, but all you really have to do is make it through the tour and you get the vouchers, without actually having to commit to buying anything. The first half of our vacations would always undoubtedly be spent doing the tours and earning our entertainment for the second half of the vacation.

Our first time-share tour of this particular holiday was set up for day two of the Florida trip. Us kids were too young to be left on our own in our hotel, so my parents dragged us along to what we all thought was a condo complex. I don't remember the name of this location, but my best guess is something like Sunset Living because upon arrival, the only people there were eighty plus in age, and those types of places are usually either called Sunrise or Sunset followed by some variation on the word *living*. If we had gone a few years later, I would've half expected one of the condos to be attached to a balloon bouquet like in *Up*. Don't get it twisted, I love the elderly; I'm just trying to paint the picture that these people were very, very old. So old that when we arrived, an ambulance was leaving with a corpse and everyone there was pretty chill about it as if it were a pizza delivery driver heading to his next stop with a pepperoni pan and a side of garlic knots. I don't know if my parents accidentally booked a retirement home tour or if this was simply old clientele, but either way, the father, son, and holy ghost of movies about old people (*The Best Exotic Marigold Hotel*/*Poms*/*Book Club*) were all likely based on this property.

Usually these tours consist of free coffee and stale chocolate chip cookies, followed by a golf cart ride where my dad would tell his life story to anyone who would listen and my mom would stealthily kick him as a signal to him to shut the fuck up. My brothers and I would try to be on our best behavior because our parents were strict, and we knew better than to act up. Usually.

A nice but erratic, thirtysomething woman was our tour guide. Her name was something like Cindy, and I'll never forget the speed and volume at which she spoke. Do you ever meet someone who asks questions at such a rapid pace, it would exhaust even the Riddler? She spent her days surrounded by old people, so that's probably why she shouted everything like she was Gerard Butler in *300*. It's likely she either drank a few too many cups of coffee or did a few too many lines of cocaine before taking our family of five on a tour of this particular retirement community, which I honestly don't even fault her for.

Cindy was a one-woman show at Sunset Living. She spent the day rotating through families, like mine, who needed free entertainment and had no intent to invest in a time-share. I imagine she grew up wanting to become an actor but instead decided to channel her BFA in theater into Sunset Living. "Every day is a performance," she would tell her boyfriend every morning when she laced up her Keds and paired them with an early-'90s power suit. I imagine all time-share tours are filled with tour de force performances, even outside of Florida, and many of the actors involved have no prior experience on stage or screen. They bring out the Meryl in the unlikeliest of candidates.

When it came time for the tour portion of the day, Cindy loaded us onto a single golf cart. I'd like you all to take a moment to imagine a golf cart. They aren't made for six people, but we didn't have a choice. We had two options: Mom or Dad could stay behind with us kids while the other parent took the tour, or we could all jam into that tiny vehicle. If one of the parents stayed back, we wouldn't get as many dinner vouchers, so that wasn't an option. Mom and Dad instead sat in the main seats next to Cindy, who acted as our driver and Orlando's own Pablo Escobar, while us three boys sat in the back seat, which faced outward at the street. Our parents listened to Cocaine Cindy shout the benefits of Sunset Living while she drove through a sea of elderly people going about their days.

At this point, Mom and Dad were distracted by Cindy the Snowman while us kids were forced to entertain ourselves. If you've never had older brothers before, it entails a lot of pushing and shoving and hitting and making fun of. There's also a lot of them grabbing your forearm and using it to punch your face while yelling, "Stop hitting yourself," as they force you to literally hit yourself. Older brothers can play that game for hours and never tire of it.

Around the five-minute mark of Junior yelling, "Stop hitting your-self," as he made me punch my own face, Mom turned around and demanded we be quiet for the rest of the ride. Just as she said it, Dad turned around with his thick, Italian eyebrows peeking out from the aviators that he got as a reward for buying enough boxes of cigarettes (the '90s were wild), which we knew meant business. My brothers and I zipped our lips and made sure our folks could hear Cindy's drug-fueled presentation over anything we were doing.

Our vow of silence didn't last long. Bryan shoved Junior, who kicked me, and I'm sure I screamed "ow!" and pissed off my Dad even more than we did before. Now's a good time to mention that we were scared of my Dad as kids. That doesn't mean we didn't love him or that he was by any means abusive; he just instilled fear in us. You didn't want to piss him off because then he would find subtle ways to ruin your life. He would assign us extra chores or take away the things we liked most. Mom was more of a softie, but Dad was tough. When we would act up in public, he would take his thumb and index finger and place it on our neck. He wouldn't squeeze very hard, but he would pointedly grasp us and stare deeply into our eyes with a look that would leave Miranda Priestley shook. When we acted up for a second time on the time-share tour, he turned around and strategically placed those two fingers on Bryan, who was closest to him, and let us know that he would drive us back to Ohio immediately if we didn't stop screwing around on this bullshit tour that we were only doing for free buffet tickets.

Bryan was terrified and I was feeling extra ornery, so I stuck my tongue out at him, laughing that he was the one who had to withstand the direct wrath of dad, but I did it quietly so no one could hear. Much like the men in Broadway's *Chicago*, he had it coming, but I was smart enough to know that if I was loud in any way, I would be next to get the infamous neck-tightening. Bryan didn't take my response well, and instead of ignoring me, he decided to push me off the moving golf cart. As I remember it, Junior also somehow joined in with the push effort, and I flew off that thing like a tumbleweed floating through the desert.

Ordinarily, I would scream and shout for help or make proper noises to express my pain, but the only thing going through my head was *be quiet,* so instead I pulled a Katy Perry and simply drifted through the wind, softly, like a plastic bag. The looks on my brother's faces were shock and awe as I came to and watched them drive out of view. Instead of telling Mom and Dad and three-bump Cindy, they decided to just be quiet and continue the tour without me.

A few moments later, I stood up and evaluated my scrapes as an older woman, Roberta, came to my rescue. She saw the entire thing and she herself was in a vehicle of her own, with curlers still in her hair and last night's bold-red lipstick and rouge smeared on her shirt sleeve. It wasn't a fancy golf cart that she was driving, just a motorized, single-person scooter. Without even so much as introducing herself, she instructed me to hop on. I'd like to say I was confused, but I wasn't. Although her wheels didn't have a seat for me, I knew she was imply- ing that I needed to get on her lap so she could haul ass and get me to my folks in their moving golf cart.

Roberta knew that I was out of options. Older people are often discarded by society, but that needs to stop. There's a knowledge that comes with living as long as someone like Roberta has and also an instinct that can't be taught. A twentysomething would have taken too much time weighing the options or trying to think of an alternative solution, but sweet Roberta knew exactly what to do without wasting any time. She knew I wouldn't have been able to catch the golf cart by my tiny, injured feet, and that if I didn't act fast, I would spend my life at Sunset Living being raised by elderly Floridians. In retrospect, I'm sure it wouldn't have been all bad to spend my adolescence with this group. I would've been like the gay man in the original pilot of *The Golden Girls* (his name was Coco, and he was later cut from the show), while the other residents would've been my Dorothy, Blanche, Rose, and Sophia. Not much would've been different than the way I actually spent my teen years—in fact, maybe the new crowd would've watched *Veronica's Closet* with me while I continued avoiding sexual situations with girls, just like I did in Ohio during my youth.

Without overthinking it, I decided to hop on Roberta and catch up to my family. I was a little rough jumping on her lap, but she didn't flinch. If you've ever seen any of the Fast and the Furious movies, you'll know the look. When Vin Diesel or Tyrese need to save one of their own during the climax, they have a look of determination in their eyes as they focus on a singular goal. That's the same look Roberta gave as she revved up her disability scooter.

I was young when this whole tour fiasco happened, so of course some details are a little blurry. Were the scrapes on my knees or arms? I'm not sure. Were my clothes ruined? Don't know. What I do remember is the unforgettable sensation of sitting on Roberta's legs. As a superfan of queen/icon/legend Sally Field, I am aware of all of her work, and that includes her Boniva commercials. If you're not familiar, Boniva is a product designed to help slow bone loss that happens when you age. Way before I would see Sally on TV teaching us about elderly bone loss, I had Roberta teach me everything I needed to know. It was like sitting in a pool of Jell-O. The truth is, we're all going to get there someday, and it shouldn't be something we're afraid to talk about. We should all be so lucky to reach such an esteemed age. At eight, you're not thinking about the aging process, and you don't realize that your body will not always be firm and tight. Hopping aboard Roberta taught me this at a very young age, and I'm forever grateful.

Roberta put the pedal to the metal, and we eventually caught up to my family. I'm sure we were moving at a snail's pace, but back then, I felt like we were in an action movie, with Roberta as the rightful hero. As I look at the cinema landscape today, I can't help but feel like we as a people are missing out on our seniors being the stars of action films (among other genres). Diane Keaton should be in a Marvel movie, and I don't mean she should be playing some young, straight, white guy's aunt. I want to see her suiting up and kicking Thanos's ass. I want to see Alfre Woodard sexing Batman before saving the world without his help, and Dianne Wiest carrying the Captain America shield. There have been enough stories about the aforementioned young, cis, white men saving the world. Let's see some other people do it.

When I finally reached my family, I hopped off Roberta and bid her adieu. If it were up to me, I would've purchased a time-share right then and there and coordinated with her on syncing up our holiday schedules. In another life, she and I are sipping skinny margaritas and watching the sunset on a beautiful Florida vacation property. They say timing is everything, and unfortunately it wasn't quite right for an eight-year-old boy and a likely-close-to-ninety woman to become life-long friends. Alas, I was reunited with my older brothers, my parents, and Cindy, who was now on her coke comedown.

We've all fallen off the metaphorical golf cart a time our two in our lives. Sometimes there's no rhyme or reason for our falls—life just decides to push us off. When you're young, you're able to rebound more quickly. You hop on the old lady and keep it moving. But the older we get, the longer it takes to get back up. You might be reading this and thinking it's a silly place for a lesson, but there's always a life lesson. Anytime you stumble, remember that there's a Roberta nearby who can help. She might not immediately come to your rescue, and you might have to go looking for her, but I promise there is someone there to help you up. It might be a stranger, or a friend, or someone in your family. You don't have to go about your falls alone. Ask for help, look for help, and catch up.

You might be wondering how pissed my parents were after this stunt we pulled. Turns out, Cindy felt terrible about how the tour transpired. She was the driver when all this went down, and I'm sure during some part of her training, they told her not to let any children fall out of the moving vehicle, and then if they do, notice when the kid flies out onto the open road. The snafu cost her a bunch of extra theme park/dinner/show vouchers, as she threw as many as she could at us to keep us quiet. I'm not sure what she thought we would do? Yelp wasn't around at that time, so the only way to voice complaints about a particular service was by word of mouth. Sure, we might go back to our hotel and tell another family that the tour we just took was led by a woman high on booger sugar who drove away as the youngest child was launched off the ride in her care, but Cindy was so booked and busy that I'm not sure a cancellation would've mattered all that much to the bottom line. We spent the rest of the vacation using up our free buffet tickets and seeing local Florida theater performances that none of us really enjoyed but went to anyway because they were free. It also allowed us the opportunity to go to the infamous Orlando parks, which had their own set of challenges...

Nickelodeon

"Don't get mad, get everything."
THE FIRST WIVES CLUB (1996)

Vacation: Day Three

The Florida vacation was in full swing when we hit the theme parks using the comped tickets we earned from the traumatic old folks' neighborhood tour. First up was Disney World, where my family lost me midmorning and didn't find me for a couple of hours. I may have been young, but I have a vivid memory of the moment I realized my family was nowhere near me. I tried to tell Pluto that I was lost, but the characters aren't supposed to talk to you, so there was a lot of miming from the adult dog. I could've gotten his autograph, but he wasn't quick to help find my parents, so he can rot. I'm sure they have some sort of protocol now, and perhaps the human inside the costume didn't even hear me, but in retrospect, whaa-aattt the fuck? Eventually I gave up asking Mickey's pet to assist me, and I found a nice couple who helped me find my folks. Now that I'm an adult, I understand child leashes. Kids run off, and it's hard to keep track of three of them for an entire day, let alone a vacation. That said, I'm not letting my mom and dad off that easily, mostly because they gaslit me for years, telling me that I didn't get lost on that trip. For years I would say, "Remember that time I got lost at Disney?" and they would respond with, "That never happened." I've since found footage of a home video where my dad admits they "misplaced" me. He never uses the word *lost*, despite the fact that I was actually more lost than Evangeline Lilly and that smoke cloud on ABC circa 2004. *Misplaced* is something that happens to your remote control when it falls underneath a couch cushion, not when one of your three children is crying and alone. I spent years thinking I had dreamed up being lost because no one would admit that it happened. The only reason I was able to confirm my suspicions is because I had those home videos transferred to digital. Watching the footage of my father's admission was satisfying but frightening. What else have I been lied to about?

For those of you keeping score at home, my childhood vacation consisted of a temper tantrum from my father after he bought a car that didn't fit in the garage, a child driving us to Florida, me getting thrown from a moving vehicle by my brothers, AND me getting "misplaced" at a theme park. Not a great trip for Danny.

After Disney, we went to Universal Studios, where things finally started to turn around for me. I spent the day on cloud nine with a *Beethoven's 2nd* plush that I got from the gift shop, alongside an autograph book signed by the likes of a Lucille Ball impersonator and an off-brand Ghostbuster. Life would've been perfect if they had someone walking around the park autographing as Bonnie Hunt's character from the aforementioned *Beethoven* sequel, but can't have it all, I suppose. Regardless, I was in pop culture heaven.

Universal Studios was also the home of Nickelodeon Studios, which was my everything at that age. *Salute Your Shorts, Hey Dude, Rugrats, Guts,* and *Double Dare* were everything to me! I even loved *Clarissa Explains It All,* starring my future archnemesis Melissa Joan Fart. MJF and I would have a fraught future, but back then, it was nothing but love.* While we were visiting Nickelodeon, they asked us to partake in a game show that was filming. I don't quite remember if it was a pilot they were shooting or simply an attraction, but there was a very high-energy young man who was hosting—we'll call him Stu—and a bunch of games set up for kids that they were filming. The Pellegrino family entered the studio and sat down in the audience. Stu introduced the show and asked for some volunteers, to which I shot my hand to the sky faster than a bolt of lightning. Stu picked me and my brother Bryan to be contestants, along with a group of about ten other kids.

They lined all of us up, Bryan and I stood next to each other, and Stu went around the horn with his microphone to introduce each child to the crowd, quickly asking everyone their names. Although Bryan and I are three years apart, we look a lot alike, particularly when we were kids. Same height, hair, and eye color. Subconsciously I was still harboring anger toward my family for what they put me through, and

---

* I don't actually have a real feud with Melissa Joan Hart. It was a joke on social media that I took too far, and now people think we hate each other despite the fact that I've never met her. I'll forever stan Aunt Hilda, Aunt Zelda, Salem, and of course, *Sabrina the Teenage Witch.* That said, I do support the idea of having a famous archnemesis without having much of a reason to hate them. It's our right.

this was my opportunity to exact some revenge, at least on one brother. So, when Stu shoved the slime-covered mic up to my mouth and asked my name, without missing a beat, I said "Bryan." As the name left my lips, I could feel the energy shift within the room. My brother, who was standing next to me, was up next, and I stole his name! He was hustled, scammed, bamboozled, hoodwinked, and led astray. He had two options. One was to say his name was Bryan and risk our entire family looking crazy. It was too obvious we were related, so what family would name two of their children the same name? His other option was to say his name was Danny, but it was all happening so fast, he couldn't quite figure it out in a socially acceptable amount of time.

Stu put the mic in front of Bryan's face, and my big brother froze. I looked up at him and saw him squirming, looking around the room for answers.

"Uh...um...uh..." Bryan said.

I glanced over at my parents and Junior, whose mouths were agape as they anxiously awaited Bryan's response.

"Um...uh..."

"What's your name?" Stu asked again.

"Uhhh..."

Then finally, after what felt like a lifetime, he said, "Danny."

Rather than going to the next kid, Stu decided to take a beat and insult my brother in front of everyone.

"Uh, are you sure?" he asked Bryan.

Bryan was humiliated, while I kicked back and smiled like a cartoon villain or Denise Richards when she sat down to do her confessional in front of a green screen on *The Real Housewives of Beverly Hills*

(#Justice4Denise). Stu was such an asshole to my brother, but I loved every second of it. They say revenge is a dish best served cold, but I like to think revenge is a public humiliation via a Nickelodeon game show pilot and a basic man named Stu insulting my brother.

Franck & Fran

"Every party has a pooper..."

FRANCK, *FATHER OF THE BRIDE PART II* (1995)

There's eccentric, and then there's Martin Short as Franck Eggelhoffer in the '90s classics *Father of the Bride* and *Father of the Bride Part II*. The performance, in my opinion, is one of the all-time greatest, an overlooked comedic role for the ages. Every year, when award nominations come out, I get upset about the iconic roles that get snubbed, sometimes because the movies themselves aren't great, and other times because the actors don't subscribe to the politics of award season. Either way, Martin Short's on-screen presence will be remembered long after most of the dramatic recipients receive their gold statues. And so will Regina Hall's performance in the Scary Movie franchise, Jennifer Elise Cox and Christine Taylor in the Brady Bunch movies, Anna Faris in everything, Lisa Kudrow and Mira Sorvino in *Romy and Michele's High School Reunion*, Joan Cusack in *Addams Family Values*, and so on. These roles may not be the most awarded, but they will all live on in memes and GIFs for an eternity, with gay men on the internet ensuring that they are never forgotten.

Franck is a personal favorite of mine for many reasons, first and foremost because those movies are comfort food in film form. Watching the Nancy Meyers/Charles Shyer flicks feels like wrapping yourself in a blanket of love on a cozy evening. When my anxiety is high, I simply need to turn on the Steve Martin movie for an instant boost of endorphins.

When I was growing up, there wasn't a lot of gay representation in media. One of the reasons I think it took me so long to come out is because I didn't see many examples of people living healthy and successful lives as out homosexuals within scripted media. When there were gay characters in film and TV, they often felt like stereotypes or the butt of the joke.

I did sketch comedy at a very popular theater in Los Angeles during my twenties, and I wrote a scene with a straight male. The two of us were playing coworkers at a company holiday party, and we couldn't figure out a way to wrap up the scene. Someone suggested that the two characters kiss at the end of the sketch, not because they were in love, but because it felt like the easiest way to go out on a laugh. I didn't want to do it, but I never spoke up and we eventually performed the lip-lock in front of a huge audience. The moment the straight actor kissed me on the lips, the crowd erupted in laughter. The sexuality became the punchline. And this was in the 2010s! They laughed because audiences have been trained to equate straight men kissing other men with comedy, whether it be on SNL when John Krasinski kissed Pete Davidson during his 2021 monologue or back in the '90s when the movie *In & Out* had Kevin Kline and Tom Selleck smooch for giggles. It's exhausting.

The Franck character is never officially revealed to be gay in *Father of the Bride*, which raises a different set of issues. Characters were frequently coded as gay because studios worried that making them outright homosexuals would be too much for viewers to handle, and many times these characterizations were written by straight people. Our community had to settle for scraps. Franck had no romantic subplot and although his assistant, played by B.D. Wong, feels like a boyfriend or partner to the audience, it's never stated as such. Even so, I still read the character as homosexual, and in this film, all the qualities that I would normally cringe at in a gay character from the era, I loved. The nuance that Martin brought transcended all the stereotyped flamboyance and gave us the most memorable role in that movie. He was messy, dramatic, had an indistinguishable accent, and favored extravagance, but it was impossible to walk away from that film not adoring Franck.

Detour

There's another F-R-A-N who has had a big impact on me...of course, I'm talking about Fran Drescher. *The Nanny* is everything to me: style guide, life guru, and a fictional character who can single-handedly save me from my own neuroses. Fran has also always been a wonderful LGBTQ+ ally. Aside from being a flawless role for Ms. Drescher, the theme song is...the greatest television theme song of all time. I'm sorry, I don't make the rules.

My appendix burst recently, and moments after arriving at the ER, a doctor told me I would need surgery to have it removed. I don't love surgery, to put it lightly. As someone who is already anxious enough, the idea of cutting me open to remove an organ is...not great. Luckily, they have drugs for people like me. Before they brought me in for the anesthesia, they loaded me with morphine and some other concoction that can only be described as heavenly. Just as the meds were kicking in, my nurses were switching shifts. As high as I was, I was still scared about going into the operating room all alone. Fortunately, I didn't have to go in solo, as one of the employees clocking in was a young woman named Fran, who swooped in and held my hand tight as I waited impatiently.

"Hi, I'm Fran, I'll be your nurse for the rest of the night," she said.

"Fran! I LOVE Fran!" I replied to a woman I'd never met. "Do you watch *The Nanny?*"

"I've seen it before."

Fran the nurse wheeled me into the operating room, where she continued to hold my hand as I met the anesthesiologist. Everything from that point on is a blur, but when I came to after they removed my appendix, Fran told me I was an A-plus patient.

"Normally when we give patients anesthesia, we have them count down from ten until they pass out. You didn't do any counting, but you did get halfway through *The Nanny* theme song—the part about style and flair—"

"She was there!" I shouted, still high as a kite.

I'm forever grateful to Fran the nurse, and all nurses, who work so tirelessly to make patients feel comfortable during those terrifying moments when we're sick and fragile inside the hospital walls.

Furthermore, I'm grateful to Fran Drescher for creating a character who is so comforting in times of need. In a full circle moment, I got a chance to tell Fran about my hospital story when she came on my show. Her warmth and humor heals.

All that's to say I love Martin Short's character and his energy. About twice a year, I rewatch the flicks and fall in love all over again. Last time I did, I walked around for about a week after shouting, "Hall-ooo!" in the cadence of my fave wedding planner, or "Motha and daughta are prognont togetha? Get out of town!" I'd do the impression for anyone who would listen, and turns out not everyone is amused by my character work.

I'm not sure if any of you have ever had pre-workout drink, a devil's powder that I can only assume is filled with a mix of caffeine, Pixy Stix, and crack cocaine, designed to give consumers the energy to lift a car when they arrive at their local Planet Fitness. For months, I had been taking a couple scoops of pre-workout before going to a group fitness class held in a dark room where they played Dua Lipa remixes for an hour. I noticed the drink was not good for someone like me who suffers from anxiety, but I still wanted something to give me a jolt before the class. Enter pre-workout gummies. Nowadays they make everything in gummy form: vitamins, melatonin, weed. The gym I went to offered me a pack of these specific gummies for $6.99, but one day they had someone giving away free samples, so I threw them in my bag and saved them for when I needed them.

One Saturday morning, I had signed up for my class (nonrefundable) and had a little mini hangover from some bed wine the night before but otherwise was in a great mood. I wish I could say that I spent Friday getting wild with some friends, but the truth is, I put a face mask on for self-care (#FaceMaskFriday), opened the bed wine while the mask dried, and then accidentally fell asleep with the mask still on. Tale as old as time. Regardless, my mini hangover was enough to dissuade me from going to the class I signed up for, and coffee wasn't doing it, so I grabbed my pre-workout energy gummies and shoved the entire pack in my mouth. I should've read the packaging. Turns out you're supposed to take one to two gummies thirty to sixty minutes before the workout. I got the timing right, but I took the entire package, which was ten to twelve actual gummies. Whooooooo! I was…A LOT. The energy hit me hard and almost immediately.

My drive to the gym was INTENSE as I sang the Pussycat Dolls' greatest hits and some '90s rap at the tippy top of my lungs. My BPM was about 574, and I began sweating more than I ever have at an actual workout. Furthermore, I'm already a terrible driver, but a mouthful of energy gummies turned me into a dangerous presence on the road. The good news is that I was alert, the bad news is that my hands were shaking, and I wanted to drive as fast as humanly possible. I was also running late, so I was texting my friend to let him know I was running late and to reserve my spot.

NEVER TEXT AND DRIVE. It's so incredibly dangerous, and I'm lucky nothing happened other than I eventually I ran a red light. It's no excuse, but I had no control over anything by this point due to the devil's candy. Hindsight is twenty-twenty. A cop saw me and turned on his lights, signaling for me to pull over.

I was scared, still shaking.

"You had your cell phone out," the officer said right when I rolled down my window.

"I'm so sorry, I—"

"And your head was bouncing everywhere," he added.

"I know, I'm sorry, I was doing some bad rapping. I'm embarrassed."

He tilted his head, raised his brows out of the top of his aviator sunglasses, and looked me right in my twitching eyes.

"I haven't done any bad wrapping since Christmas," he said, just missing a *bad um chhh* sound effect.

I took this to believe that he and I now had a rapport. He made a little gift wrap joke, and although he didn't smile after he said it, it was definitely a joke, right? It was enough for me to exhale for the first time since I saw his lights going off.

"Can I see your license and registration?" he asked.

I handed the man my license and searched my glove compartment for my registration. There were papers everywhere, a stack of things I shoved inside. My car is a hot mess, so he stood there, waiting for me to find the forms. After what felt like forty-five minutes, I finally found my registration, and because I thought we had a comedic relationship, I let out a very loud and aggressive, "Haallll-oooo!" a la Franck Eggelhoffer.

He gave me a familiar look, one that said, "What the F are you doing?"

"That's my Franck," I explained.

"Who?" he asked.

"From *Father of the Bride*. Franck."

No response. He simply walked away and wrote up my ticket. Maybe I should've written him a ticket for not knowing *Father of the Bride*. I never made it to the workout class, instead deciding I already missed too much of it and my time would be better spent going home to watch a movie. As I looked at my collection, I noticed there were more options of flicks with LGBTQ+ characters than there were back when I first watched Martin Short as Mr. Eggelhoffer, characters who were allowed to be outright homosexuals and sometimes even the star of their own stories. Still, I wonder when there will be a big budget action movie with a gay lead, or an animated feature with lesbians who have more than one line of dialogue. I feel for all the minorities who have yet to see themselves as the heroes and villains and wedding planners and stylish nannies onscreen. I'll continue to plead and fight for more robust representation, and in the meantime, I'll celebrate the Francks and Frans we've loved along the way.

The Shawl

"Is this chicken what I have, or is this fish? I know it's tuna, but it says 'chicken by the sea.'"

—JESSICA SIMPSON

I would like to take a moment to talk A Little Bit™ about a story that's Irresistible™. Jessica Simpson released a memoir called *Open Book*. When the paperback came out, she included real entries from her journal. Before we go any further, I'd like to do the same...

Dear Diary,

Dolly Parton, Tom Hanks...there are but a handful of universally liked celebrities, the kind of people who the mere mention of will elicit a smile, a fond memory. Through extensive pop culture research, I've found that Queen Jessica Simpson is one of those people. Her case is interesting because her biggest professional success is her clothing line, which isn't as flashy or in-your-face as music or acting is. Jess has done both of those other things—and done them well I might add—but her true appeal is her relatability.

I first fell in love with her during the early pop years. She entered the music scene with a grocery store anthem called "I Wanna Love You Forever." To this day, it's rare to be in the frozen pizza section picking up a DiGiorno without hearing her belt about cherishing every drop on her knees, a troubling lyric to say the least. I think many gay men (or rather, closeted young boys) of that era became obsessed with the invisible pop princess wars that plagued TRL. Come to think of it, I think it was the media once again pitting women against each other. The truth is, they were all amazing. Britney was always number one, as she arrived on the scene first and garnered the most attention. Many people discount Britney as a vocalist, but I always thought she was incredibly talented in that department. Specifically, there's a quality about Britney's phrasing that is unparalleled, but that's a tale for another time. Christina was the number two, never quite reaching the heights of Brit-Brit, but an enormous talent with stunning pipes. I'll never forget the VH1 Behind the Music where Christina's version of "Reflection" is discussed and her ability to hit a high E above middle C. Every other singer was shook.

The third slot was a tug of war between Jess and Mandy Moore. Mandy seemed to inch ahead during the Walk to Remember era, but I think Jessica was winning during that time she did a song with her then-boyfriend N*ck L*ch*y for the Here on Earth soundtrack (PS remember Leelee Sobieski? SOS on Leelee).

Although Jessica "Irresistible" Simpson and Mandy "I Wanna Be with You" Moore were neck and neck, they were always just a beat behind Xtina "Dirrty" Aguilera and Britney "I'm Not a Girl, Not Yet a Woman" Spears. That is, until Newlyweds, which changed the course of history forever.

The year was 2003. iTunes had just launched, The Lizzie McGuire Movie took the box office by storm (by storm, I mean I personally saw it in theaters more than once), Mike Myers made us all feel like we were on acid with his live-action Cat in the Hat film, and the whale from Free Willy passed. It's also the year MTV debuted one of their most popular shows of all-time, starring Jessica and her new husband N*ck L*ch*y, whom she had married in October of 2002.

Jess and N*ck seemed like a match made in heaven, and combining their star power catapulted them to that top spot in the early aughts. When that first episode of Newlyweds aired, audiences were hungry for celeb-reality. The Osbournes had become a huge hit, but there weren't many other shows that showcased celebrities in the same way. People who loved Ozzy and Sharon could now get their fix from a newly married couple, and years before social media would give fans access to the personal lives of the rich and famous, MTV was there.

That first episode is shocking upon re-watch. Nowadays, reality shows have more of a narrative structure, and the production value is similar to that of scripted fare. If you put on The Real Housewives on Bravo, you'll notice the cast members are always mic'ed, with full hair and makeup in most of their scenes. Back then it was more casual with multiple scenes of Jess and N*ck at chain restaurants.

Newlyweds *catapulted them onto the A-list. Suddenly they were everywhere, but Jess seemed to get the bigger professional boost. Her music career, which at that time was fledgling a bit, was now bigger than ever. They re-released one of her albums, "With You" became a radio smash, and she started moving lots of merch, my favorite being the lickable dessert beauty line. There's an infamous episode of* Newlyweds *where Jessica gets a stomachache filming the promo for the line and struggles to finish the shoot. Memories.*

By the end of Newlyweds, *you could tell the two did not care for each other. The final episode was about the couple moving into a bigger house and reflecting on their time. They never actually moved into another house together, and their reflecting was a way to wrap the series as quickly as possible while filming as little as possible with each other.*

*They went their separate ways, and I had to learn to accept it. N*ck finally had a hit in "What's Left of Me," which was about the dissolution of his relationship, and it's also a video that features his now-wife. Jessica didn't have a huge post-breakup song like he did (#Justice4IBelongToMe), but she did have something even better ahead of her...a billion-dollar fashion empire.*

During the Newlyweds *era, Jessica's sister Ashlee also rose to fame on her own MTV show. Destined to be a star, her first single catapulted her onto the A-list alongside Jess. It's rumored (by me only) that the Hemsworth brothers modeled their career after the success of the Simpson siblings. The two sisters even sang a duet*

of "The Little Drummer Boy" at an ABC variety hour that I will
NEVER, ever forget...

We're going to have to stop there. The publisher tells me that this book
is supposed to be focused on my life and also that they didn't pay me to
write an oral history of the Simpson family. (NOTE: I'm open to doing
one of those if the $ is right, and even maybe if the $ isn't.)

Okay, back to me...the MTV *Newlyweds* era was truly fabulous,
not just because of the story lines or performances but because of the
fashions. I'm not a fashionista; every time I leave the house I worry
a morning show will ambush makeover me, but I do know about
the massive style influence Jessica had in the aughties. There was, of
course, her multicolored Louis Vuitton bag, the Ken Paves hairstyling,
and my personal favorite...the legendary yellow shawl.

The shawl was worn throughout the entire series, and Jess also
had an alternate version that she wore on tour in the early aughts. It
was so beloved, I dedicated an Instagram post to the piece, with hundreds of people commenting about how much they loved it too. I even
remember when it aired, so many of the girls in my high school tried
to pull off a similar look, but most of them just looked like they draped
their grandma's afghans over their teenage shoulders.

Thousands of likes later, Cecilia De Bucourt—the designer of the
shawl—reached out to me via DM to thank me for spotlighting her
creation. I was honored that she was messaging me, and she could
NOT have been nicer. She asked if I would want her to send me one,
telling me they are all handmade, so each one looks a little bit different,
but she would get it to look as close to Jessica's as she could. As much

as I love to get free stuff, I live in a small apartment and don't have a ton of space for extras, but I could not say no to this opportunity. I sent the designer my PO box address, and a few days later, it arrived!

My PO box doesn't have ample parking for patrons, but I was able to find a spot on a busy West Hollywood street. I went in to get my mail and was so excited to see the package with the designer listed on the return address. I ripped it open and marveled at my new ladies' statement piece, which looked almost exactly like the one on *Newlyweds*.

As I walked back to my car, I was on such a high that I decided to treat myself to a doughnut from a nearby shop. I gently tossed the shawl into the front seat along with my other mail and headed to pick up a half dozen of the most delicious blueberry and glazed in Los Angeles (Tasty Donuts on Santa Monica). Nothing better than a doughnut, especially when they're fresh, perfectly crispy on the outside, and pillowy on the inside, with a sweet sugar glaze.

After I picked up the snack, I once again headed back to my car. From afar, I noticed a man at my passenger door, with a crowbar that he was using to, seemingly, break into my vehicle.

I wish I could tell you that I was concerned he was stealing my mail or planning to hot-wire my car, but the truth is the only thing that came to mind was that my *Newlyweds* shawl was resting in the front seat. Who knows if I would be able to get another that looked as good as the one I got in the mail that day! Maybe I could've paid for another, but I didn't have tons of money to be spending on women's clothing that was popular in 2004.

"HEY! GET AWAY FROM MY JESSICA SIMPSON SHAWL!" I shouted as I ran toward the man breaking into my car.

I've never been a fighter. I mean, I'm not much of a lover either, but I certainly don't want to come in contact with anyone dangerous, and yet there I was, running to someone brave enough to break into a stranger's car in the *middle of the day*. Not only that, but as I got closer, I noticed that he was a very strong-looking man, albeit on the shorter side, which I tend to like. He had white hair and a beard, with huge biceps bursting out of his red T-shirt. Looking like a hot, miniature Santa that could kick my ass would normally turn me on more than I can express in words, but I was pissed and preparing myself to fight little Saint Nick.

"That's my car!" I continued, "and my *Newlyweds* shawl!"

The man looked up and noticed me running toward him. (Well, I'm not sure that I was running as much as I was shuffling and trying not to lose any of my fresh doughnuts.) Unfortunately, it was all for naught, as the flimsy box holding my fried dough decided to give out on my way to save my mustard shoulder draping. We honestly need doughnut box reform because they jam them inside a box that looks like it's stapled together with construction paper. A gust of wind would tear that thing apart, so there was no safe way to run with a box like that. The dough-nuts fell to the ground one by one as I got closer to my Honda, and I was devastated. I stopped briefly to consider picking them off the dirty road, but ultimately decided not to when I remembered that one time I saw a used condom on the ground outside my PO box.

"Get away from my *Newlyweds* shawl! It's one-of-a-kind!" I screamed louder, this time even more intimidating, weaponizing the devastation of losing my donuts to the sex-stained concrete.

Santa wiggled his crowbar out of my window and ran like hell away from me like I was a child catching him eating my cookies on Christmas Eve night.

Knowing the shawl was safe, I slowed down to catch my breath. I eventually made my way to the car and was relieved to see my yellow statement piece safely in the passenger seat where I had left it.

When I got home, I recounted the events to my boyfriend, explaining that this man was trying to steal my famous shawl.

"He was probably trying to steal your car," my boyfriend said.

"No, he was at the passenger window, not the driver's side," I assured him.

"Did you have any other mail?" he asked.

"Well, yeah, just a few letters that I picked up with the gift...and my phone was in the car with it because I accidentally left it in there."

"So he was trying to steal your phone," my boyfriend said.

"You don't get it. You obviously just don't get it. It's *the* yellow shawl from *Newlyweds*. That's what he wanted," I explained.

"If he was breaking in during the middle of the day, risking getting caught by someone, anyone, in the neighborhood, I assure you that he wasn't trying to get your sweater," he said.

"It's a SHAWL! FROM MTV! And I wish I didn't catch him because I bet next Christmas, you would've seen him wearing it when he delivered presents to our house," I playfully, albeit also angrily, added.

My boyfriend rolled his eyes at me while I went to the other room to watch TV. As I sat down to watch *The View*, a breeze came in from the open door of our living room. Luckily, I had my *Newlyweds* shawl to keep me warm.

Sun Will Rise

I wanted to die just a handful of years ago. Writing that makes my hands shake and my heart race. The idea is so disparate from the smiley, Midwest persona I give off, and I'm scared to even tell you more because somehow discussing it makes it feel even more real. Will you see me differently now? Will the rest of my words hold less weight in comparison? Only now, in hindsight, can I see that my mental health struggles are part of my story but not my entire story.

By now you might be wondering about my dark side. Everyone has one. Kelly Clarkson even released a song called "Dark Side" that wasn't quite the hit it should've been (#Justice4DarkSide), but it was proof that even Queen Kelly has some demons. My dark side comes in the form of depression and anxiety that rear their ugly heads quite often. As a lover of reality television, I typically enjoy the type of shade that comes from the mouth of a Real Housewife, but there's another kind of shade in my life that's more difficult to endure; there's a pitch-black cloud that drifts over me and covers all the light every once in a while that I'd be remiss not to talk about with all of you.

Never was that cloud darker than a fateful drive to "the happiest place on earth."

When most people talk about mental health, it's often through language like *light* and *dark*, and *sun* and *clouds*. By now we should have a better way of describing the inner turmoil one goes through in life, but we don't, or specifically, I don't. I find the easiest—and best—way is through the type of words that you would find in the journal of an emo mid-aughts teen who wore *Nightmare Before Christmas* clothes year-round, so bear with me here. I'm a generally happy person, but there are times in my life when the anxiety and depression seep into my everyday existence and crush me, most recently just a few weeks ago, but it's been happening on and off for years, with one particularly no good, very bad experience.

I first struggled with anxiety when I was nineteen years old. That's a tough age for anyone, but I was stuck in the closet in small-town Ohio. Up until then, I ignored my sexuality or swept it under the rug. Sure, at fourteen, the hand-me-down jeans I wore to sneak into *Cruel Intentions* were forced to accommodate a boner anytime Ryan Phillippe showed up on screen, but I was able to convince myself that I was straight. By nineteen, I was having much more trouble convincing myself. Side note: I know I'm gay because I was able to spell *Phillippe* right on one try, while *accommodate* took me three tries.

The anxiety started when I realized I would either have to come out of the closet or live a life of lies. As I bought myself time, the anxiety started to manifest in physical symptoms. My skin began to break out, my blood would itch, I couldn't catch my breath, and panic attacks started becoming more and more frequent. Eventually, I made an appointment with my primary care doctor when a skin rash developed. The doctor checked me out, asked me just a few basic questions, did some blood work, recommended a therapist that I did *not* see, and diagnosed me with anxiety before I left the exam room. He prescribed me some pharmaceuticals and sent me on my way.

By the time I turned twenty-one, I thought I had the anxiety under control. At twenty-two, I officially came out of the closet to friends and family, and I assumed my struggles were over. I would get the occasional panic attack, which I learned to treat with a low dose of Xanax, but other than that, I *felt* in control of my emotions. Spoiler alert: I wasn't.

January 2015 was when I hit my low point. That's when depression entered the group chat. I've experienced sadness before, but this was something new, and it was unfathomable to me. When people talk about depression, they often use it as an adjective to describe a rough breakup period, or a time of despair. It's often thrown out into the wild during any old casual conversation...

"I'm sorry, we don't have french fries, but I can get you a side salad."

"Ugh, no fries? I'm so depressed."

I'm guilty myself of throwing it around without meaning it, but I'm here to tell you that depression is so much more than a lack of fries. It's debilitating.

I think back to that time and I try to put the puzzle pieces together to see the bigger picture of how I got to be the way that I am. I wonder if the depression was always in me, dormant and waiting to say hello, or did a string of events cause some sort of a mental break? I'm still working on figuring all this out, so forgive me if I'm leaving certain things vague. All I know for certain is that 2015 is when my life outlook changed forever, and I'll never forget the day it all came to a head on my way to, of all places, a theme park.

Leading up to that January, I had some setbacks. I had just lost my grandma and, like I mention in another chapter, I held on to a lot of guilt about not seeing her toward the end of her life. I was also struggling to find work and was leaning toward giving up chasing my dreams. Nothing was working for me professionally, and top of all of that, I was also twenty-fucking-eight, which I read is a historically difficult year to go through. Regardless of this (Lemony Snicket) series of unfortunate events, I suddenly found myself struggling in a way I wasn't prepared or equipped for.

A wave of sadness came over me, and the world seemed a little darker. I felt alone. I wasn't actually alone, mind you. My immediate family lived in Ohio and I resided in California, but they were always a phone call away, and I had really wonderful friends and a boyfriend who loved me within walking distance. Unfortunately, when I would think about those friends or family that loved me, the depression would morph my memories of those people into graphic novel–style villains. In reality, they were still in my corner, but the depression manifested itself into hallucinations. I couldn't see the kindness in my best friends' eyes, I couldn't believe the support that came from my boyfriend, and my parents looked like monsters to me, even just in memory. It might sound like I'm being metaphorical, but in my case, I would close my eyes and when I would think of or picture those people closest to me, the depression would visualize them in a different way than I had ever thought of them before. Even the memory of my dear grandma would be completely distorted. I knew they were all there for me, but the disease convinced me otherwise. Depression doesn't want you to see good, it wants you to see the world as a dark and scary place, a place you no longer want to be a part of, and those feelings snowball. Depression is like a tiny dark cell in your body that multiplies faster than you can catch it.

Initially I didn't even want to get out of bed, struggling even to make it to the shower every day. There would be days in a row where I wouldn't leave my bed. When I started to notice this negativity sweep my body, I did everything I could to fight it off. I worked out harder, I meditated longer, drank herbal tea. Sounds silly, but if I had even once heard something was "good for mental health," I would try it. I was fortunate enough to have the resources to do these things, but they weren't a cure-all. Regardless, it was too little, too late (#Justice4Jojo). The cell had multiplied, and I couldn't control it anymore. That was when I realized I had to learn to understand the depression so I could live with it.

I noticed around that time that I was also scared of the way my mind was working. I was self-aware enough to know that I wasn't well but unsure of how to go about helping the cause outside of those commonly known tools like journaling or acupuncture. This fear caused me to want to stay exclusively in what I call my safety zones, or places I was familiar with: my home, my gym, my grocery store. If I traveled outside those safety zones, I was in a constant state of panic that I would somehow crumble to dust. The anxiety was now working in conjunction with the depression...two pieces of shit doing everything they could to ruin my life.

When I finally admitted I had a problem, I told my boyfriend, who thought it would be a good idea to go to Disneyland. Lol. We live close by and that, in the moment, seemed like a great place to be to fight off the feelings inside. Maybe forced happiness isn't the best idea when you're at a low point, but whatever, they have chocolate-covered peanut butter balls you can buy at Pooh's Corner, and I was desperate, so we hopped in a car and made our way to Anaheim to see Mickey Mouse. About ten minutes into the car ride, I began worrying about being away from those safety zones I told you about.

I looked out the window as we were driving, and my eyes were seeing the other vehicles on the road smashing into us and driving off the freeway to a free fall. I looked over at my boyfriend for some comfort, and he looked evil to me. More hallucinations. Remember in *Batman Begins* when Scarecrow sprays that fear gas and suddenly Batman's face morphs into a crazy, claylike shape? That's what I was seeing, minus a supporting turn from Katie Holmes. Just writing about it still makes me feel uneasy. I had never heard of this type of symptom before! My imagination saw darkness where there was light, and once these thoughts came into my head, I couldn't stop them. I was self-aware enough to know that the cars weren't actually driving themselves off the freeway and that my boyfriend loved me more than anything, but that's what I was seeing. Crashing, one by one. Evil all around me. And knowing what you're seeing is not reality can cause a lot of hysteria. My breath got heavy and fast, and I felt my chest collapsing while I rode passenger. If you've never experienced a panic attack, I hope you never do. It's sort of like when you stand up too quickly and your line of vision gets blurry, but you also can't catch your breath and it feels like you're dying. THEY ARE NOT FUN. I tried everything to stop the thoughts and slow down my breathing. I put headphones in my ears and did a ten-minute guided meditation on my iPhone, which calmed me down enough to not feel like I was going to drop dead on the spot.

My boyfriend pulled into a gas station and got out of the car. I can't remember if I told him to get out so I could have some space or if he just did it instinctively. All I could do in that moment was focus on my breathing and let one inhale lead me to the next exhale. "Deep breath in. Hold it. Breathe out," I said to myself. Repeat. "Deep breath in. Hold it. Breathe out." I continued this until my heart rate steadied. One time I read that a normal resting heart rate is 60 to 100 beats per minute in adults, so when my heart is racing, I say, "Fifty-nine BPM," over and over to myself. I'm not even sure it's medically accurate, but I visualize my heart beating just a hair slower than average, and when I calm down enough to feel like I hit 59 beats per minute, I can move forward. I don't actually measure my heart rate, although I should, I simply use it as a mantra to calm me down. Something to focus my thoughts and clear the swirling vortex in my head.

At around 59 beats per minute, my boyfriend got back into the driver's seat and we made the ridiculous decision to continue our drive to Disney. LOL again. I wanted to go home, but I pushed through because he was doing this for me, and we were closer to the park than we were to home. Did I mention I'm not great at decision-making? Once we entered the grounds, I put on the happy face that was expected of me, but beneath the surface, I was in a living hell. There's a picture of me at the park from that day, in front of the big, magic castle, smiling in

my *DuckTales* shirt next to my loving boyfriend. Anyone would look at it and think
I was having the time of my life, but when
I see it, I remember the pain and fear that
existed behind my eyes. I remember the
hallucinations and the panicked breath of
the drive to Disney. It was like that movie
Inside Out, only my little cartoon emotions
were running around headquarters like

chickens with their heads cut off, all the while sirens are blaring.

Early on in the visit, my boyfriend excused himself to the restroom
and I cried to myself, wondering how I would make it through the rest
of the day he planned. I was both scared and sad. An older woman saw
me crying as she waited for her husband to finish up in the restroom,
and she asked if I was okay. I put my sunglasses on and told her I was
just *so* happy to be there. I pretended the tears were of joy, and I got
away with it because she didn't know the difference between my sad
eyes and my happy ones. There are only a handful of friends I've had
in my life for years, and they know my looks so well that they would've
probably known how I felt before I knew how I felt. That's the beauty
of a long-term friend. I somehow tricked everyone into thinking I was
having a good time that day, even the camera, but inside I couldn't wait
to get home, back to my safety zone.

Later on in the day, I excused myself to the restroom, where I
locked the door and forced myself to throw up as a way to control
emotions that were uncontrollable. The only other time I felt semi-
normal was when we rode on Space Mountain, a roller coaster that is

superfast and mostly in the dark. I normally hate rides, but something about the speed and lights off made it feel like the outside world was catching up with the way I felt on the inside. As soon as it was over, the tiny relief wore off. Nothing else I did helped, not the corn dog I usually find so satisfying and not a wave from Goofy himself. The pain that day was so strong on the inside that despite the beauty around me, I simply no longer wanted to live inside my body.

I hit my low. People who suffer from migraines often get something called *postdrome* that happens after the main migraine, kind of like a migraine hangover. I think of that theme park visit as my low point, but the trauma lingered. The immobilizing darkness and hallucinations lasted about a month longer. I wasn't healed after that month, but I was starting to notice some changes in my mood.

This all led me to (finally) seeing a therapist, which was the final piece of the puzzle on my road to recovery. I should've done it sooner. She taught me that those thoughts I was having on the way to Disneyland of the cars on the freeway were the depression trying to normalize suicide. Up until then, I thought my depression wasn't bad because I didn't ever explicitly think of killing myself. I figured the feeling of not wanting to live was somehow unrelated because I hadn't thought about explicitly inflicting pain upon myself. Turns out, it all just looked a little different than what I expected. In a weird way, I was trying to cover. I convinced myself that suicide never entered the picture, even though deep down, I knew that it did. Sometimes our bodies and minds try to protect us by making us forget our own stories. Plus, depression is able to twist realities in ways you could never anticipate. Ever since that trip to Disneyland, I've spent so much time learning about my brain and doing everything I can to keep that rain cloud away from me, and it hasn't stopped coming, but it comes less frequently. Sometimes I can keep it in check holistically, and other times I need a boost from prescribed medication.

Detour

The previously mentioned Queen Kelly Clarkson has a song for everything. I mentioned "Dark Side," but she also has hits like "Stronger (What Doesn't Kill You)," and "Invincible," and "Piece by Piece," and countless others to help someone when they're down. Her discography is inspirational bop after inspirational bop, alongside a steady stream of angry breakup tracks, grocery store anthems, and gorgeous ballads. One of the lesser-known non-singles is a song called "The Sun Will Rise." It's not quite the earworm that something like "Since You've Been Gone" is, but it's a cheesy midtempo bop that I play when I need some inspiration. She sings alongside Kara DioGuardi, and the lyrics move me every time. Even if you don't like the music, you might be able to appreciate the beautiful words.

Just like a longtime lover, the dark times don't come as frequently as they once did, but they still come. I've accepted that depression and anxiety will always live inside of me. However, I now have the tools to cohabit. Anyone who comes into my life, for the rest of my life, will also have to reconcile with the demons that forever reside in my home. When I close my eyes and only see dark clouds, that depression monster, I remind myself that blue skies are beyond those rain clouds and a light will shine again. I've pushed them away before, and I'll just have to keep doing it again, and again, and again, and again, and...

I can keep going because I know the sun will rise even when the dark of night feels tangled in time. The sun will always rise.

Christmas in June

I LIVE for Christmas. It's my favorite time of year, and I wish I could say that my season is kicked off with the Macy's Thanksgiving Day Parade—which, by the way, is the only place on TV that you can see something like Trishelle from *The Real World* on a Jennie-O float, singing "Up on the Housetop" with the California Raisins—but the truth is I listen to holiday music and watch *The Family Stone* year-round. Twinkle lights make me happy! Still, I recognize that the cheer is not for everyone.

I've written about many of my awkward moments in this book, but I couldn't possibly include everything. There was the time I accidentally got my envelopes mixed up before I mailed them out and I sent my newly widowed relative a card that said, "I know you would prefer a big fat ass, but this card will have to do," while my bestie got a birthday card that said, "Sorry for your loss. Praying for you." And we'll have to wait until the next book for me to really dive deep about when I applied for an internship at a music company back in the early 2000s and spelled my name with punctuation in place of the vowels to be more like P!nk. Needless to say, D@nny Pllgr!n0 didn't get the job. Or the time I accidentally ate cupcakes that expired thirteen years back on IG Live. But I'd be remiss to leave out a pivotal awkward moment regarding my year-round Christmas love.

When I moved into the apartment I'm at now, I got fancy and hired a cleaning person to come. I love *The Real Housewives*, and sometimes I learn good lessons from them, and other times I learn the bad stuff through television osmosis. The bad lesson seeped in and I was living outside my means, like so many of the women do, by paying for a service that I didn't need, but at least it meant I was getting my place dusted. I reasoned that it became part of my self-care routine. Self-care is a great excuse for bad decisions you want to make. Leaving for an hour once a month and coming back to cleanliness helped me de-stress.

The woman I hired was named Martha, and she was an odd gal who would come over and put Pop-Tarts in my freezer so she could snack on one frozen on her way home. She also had a stomach issue that caused her to, how do I put this nicely…Martha would dirty my toilet with her bowels after scrubbing it down. I don't think the frozen treat and bathroom breaks were related, but it happened regularly, and I couldn't get mad because she was so sweet. Like a baby angel. On one particular Martha visit in late June, I forgot that she was scheduled, and I was playing on the computer when she arrived. I put the screen to sleep and let her in. Immediately, she noticed some new electronics I had at the house. My boyfriend is a techie, and he is constantly upgrading and buying those home speakers that talk to you and the cleaning robots. The speakers all work in tandem with the computers, although they all seem to have different names and functions, so if you're listening to something in one room, you're listening in all the rooms. Martha right away noticed the machine that vacuums the floor and the one that mops, our own little Rosey from *The Jetsons*. I'm frankly tired of all this technology, and I assured her they don't clean as good as a human.

Martha then told me to get the F out of the house so she could clean in peace, so I grabbed my e-reader and went to sit by the communal pool that my unit overlooks for my quiet time.

When I got to the space, I noticed a twentysomething neighbor on another pool chair, relaxing from the stresses of her life with a frozen cocktail in one hand and a Jenny McCarthy book in the other. The best part about living in California is the weather. Sunshine can totally change your mood, lifting your spirits and boosting your serotonin levels. As the rays hit my face, I released the energy I'd been holding in all week. I could finally take a deep breath and it felt good to know that I'd return to a spotless living space. Before I even fired up Kelly Cutrone's book on my Kindle, I closed my eyes and bathed in the moment. Bliss.

Only a few seconds passed before I heard a familiar sound. It was two men having sex. I may not be a great contestant on *Name That Tune*, but I can certainly identify the moans of homosexual intercourse. I giggled to myself and glanced over at my neighbor, who heard it too. She smiled and looked around to try to find where the sound was coming from as the sex noises continued.

"Is that Brysen and Blake?" I said to myself, quietly identifying the thrusts as a smut film that I'm...*whispers* mildly familiar with.

Before I could get confirmation, I heard something else I recognized, only this sound was more family friendly. It was the one and only Miss Piggy, one of the greatest characters of all time, singing her rendition of "Santa Baby," originally made famous by Eartha Kitt in the 1950s.

"Is that Miss Piggy singing a Christmas song?" my neighbor asked.

"I think it might be," I replied, pretending to barely know that it was a Muppet, "AND GAY PORN!" I shouted back to her over the sounds of sleigh bells and two Sean Cody models violently sweating.

We both laughed and looked around the complex. Who could possibly be listening to Christmas music and watching gay porn in the middle of a summer workday?

Turns out, it was me. The sounds were coming from inside my house.

"Shit!" I said to the neighbor, "THAT'S MY APARTMENT!"

I frantically hopped up from my chair and did my best to slide my toes back into my cheap flip-flops. Perhaps if I had spent less money on someone cleaning, I would've been able to afford more durable summer shoes, but I digress.

When I got back into my home, I saw Martha holding one of the multiple speakers that was playing both the carol and porn at full volume. Behind her was my twenty-four-inch desktop computer showcasing the two young gentlemen who were taking turns being inside of each other, coincidentally also at a pool. Martha's eyes were wide as she tried to turn the volume down, but instead she continued to turn it up. The entire apartment building could now hear two of the more commonly played items on my computer.

I grabbed the speaker from Martha's hands, but quickly realized I too didn't know how to use it. Without being able to turn it down, I decided I needed to go right to the source. I immediately paused the video player, freezing Brysen and Blake in a compromising position, and doing so just made the Muppet music come in more clearly. I couldn't find the app that was playing the song, but I realized it had to be my Spotify account, specifically my "An Iconic Christmas" playlist.

Everything was happening so fast, I couldn't tell if it was the Alexa machine in charge of the music or the Google one that it was originating from. Did Siri have my Spotify linked? I DIDN'T KNOW HOW TO STOP IT. I went through each machine, heart racing, just trying to halt the felt diva from getting to another chorus. My vision blurred and Martha could see I was panicked. It wasn't just her either, the music was loud, but I could sense someone else was near. It was my neighbor, looking through my window, now with her roommate. Together they cupped their head against the glass and squinted in to see me nervously shaking in front of Martha and a paused gay porn scene as a pig sang about hurrying down a chimney in June.

Martha, bless her soul, took matters into her own hands and unplugged all the speakers from the wall outlets. Time stood still as I gathered my thoughts. There was no proper way to explain porn open my computer or that I listened to holiday music in the summer. Instead I just handed Martha her check early along with an extra tip, telling her to not worry about finishing the gig.

"Let's never speak of this again," I said.

She grabbed the not-yet-frozen Pop-Tart from the freezer and headed on her way as I closed the curtains on my nosy neighbors.

"Happy Gay Pride Month," she said earnestly as she left.

The next time Martha came to clean, she brought her own speaker and played music while she scrubbed the kitchen. She typically listened to soft rock when I left, that is, until her December cleaning, which would, unfortunately, be one of her last.

"Merry Christmas, Danny!" she cheerfully exclaimed when she arrived.

"You too, Martha," I replied.

Sadly, she then informed me that she would no longer be able to clean, as she was moving out of the state. Right before I left her to her last cleaning, she turned on her own gadget, and I heard a familiar sound. It was Kermit's one true love singing "Santa Baby."

"This version is my favorite now," Martha said with a chuckle.

It warmed my heart to know she got something more valuable

than money from that summer cleaning. My holiday wish every year since is that Martha went on her life journey and not only explored *The Muppets: A Green and Red Christmas* album but also found the timeless work of Brysen.

Detour

"And you don't support other women. You don't acknowledge anybody for anything they do. And as soon as Carole left the party, you talked behind her back. So how have you the ORDACITY to talk to me like you're talking to me? How about you didn't even give Dorinda credit for getting the nutcracker?"

—RAMONA SINGER, *THE REAL HOUSEWIVES OF NEW YORK*

I've watched a LOT of Bravo television. I'm talking hours and hours of footage of wealthy or wealthy-pretending women arguing over dinners, in front of psychics, and while in downward dog position with a goat on their back (I'm ready for us to collectively retire goat yoga). I've seen numerous cast combinations fighting at ax-throwing locales, and those weird rage rooms where people throw tantrums on yard sale junk. One thing I know for sure, when it comes to *The Real Housewives* franchise, even those silly moments can teach us valuable info.

From Sonja Morgan I learned to always be the straw that stirs the drink; Dr. Wendy taught me to always address a doctor correctly, sweetie; and Taylor Armstrong showed me what to do when enough is enough. Sometimes important questions are raised, like when Kathy Hilton finally brought up something that should be on all our minds... who is Hunky Dory? Because of this TV franchise, I know that when it comes to romantic entanglements, it's important to find a man who emotionally fulfills you (KNOW THAT) and also fills your love tank. Family should be thick as thieves and never steal your goddamn house. In career, it's imperative to align yourself with companies that aren't antiquated, to support other women, and to not announce your new business venture until it's ready to be released (September/spring/summer is not a specific enough date). There are ideas big and small hidden in every episode, in particular when it comes to toxic friendships and protecting your emotional space.

On the season one finale of *The Real Housewives of Salt Lake City*, Meredith Marks is talking to Jen Shah, who had been talking about Meredith's marriage behind her back throughout the season. When Jen pulls her aside to apologize for her actions, Meredith responds with, "I need to protect my positive space, and I don't have room for the negativity right now." She disengaged. Most of us in Meredith's position would instinctively accept Jen's apology and then continue the cycle, but Meredith took the road less traveled. That is DEEP. We are fragile beings, and allowing too much negative energy will break us if we allow it in.

The Real Housewives are, of course, meant to be enjoyed with a glass of wine and some friends, but don't miss the lessons. While these women can be dramatic and unpredictable, they are also a reflection of our own lives. They are the mirror. Every so often, I look around at my people and take stock of the relationships around me to decide if they are good for me. The people on-screen might not be able to completely distance themselves from the toxicity around them without actually leaving the show and the paycheck behind, but the rest of us can.

A Star Is...in the Theater?

"Hey!"

"What?"

"I just wanted to take another look at you."

A STAR IS BORN (2018)

Every year on my birthday, a sense of melancholy washes over me that is not easily rid of. I spend the days and week before wondering if I'm metaphorically behind in life. Did I accomplish all the things I wanted to by the age I'm at? No. Is my life set up the way I hoped it would be by this age? Never. Sometimes I feel like Super Mario in one of the water levels, frantically paddling through, dodging the devil fish and occasionally gasping for air. I'm sure everyone feels this way, but looking around in your thirties and seeing old friends and family on social media with their fancy houses and babies, it's hard not to feel less than. Less than because I don't own a house, less than because I have no kids, and less than because I don't have abs. I feel judged by my peers, and all the while I'm scrolling IG and judging the celebrities on my feed with a leftover Roadside Slider from the Cheesecake Factory in my free hand. It's a vicious circle of judgment. When the big birthday finally arrives every year, I'm already in such a low state that very little could bring me out of my funk, and this makes it impossible for the people around to properly celebrate me each October. Not enough attention and I absolutely sink into a deep despair that leaves me feeling broken, but too much attention and I emotionally snap, tears suddenly flowing like dough bursting out of one of those barely cracked Pillsbury cans. My loved ones can't win. Pay attention to me, but don't pay any attention to me at all. Look at me, then look away. It's not just an adult thing either, because celebrating the passing of time never sat right with me, even in my youth.

I spend most birthdays doing the same thing...dinner and a movie. Simple and easy for all involved. Food is the spot of my choice, either just with my boyfriend or a small group of my inner circle. I let them pay for me, but I am adamant that we don't do the "happy birthday" song and dance with the servers at the restaurant. I hate that. Just bring out the slice of cake and spare me the workers' *The Voice* audition because I'm certainly not turning around my chair if I hear an off-key melody from someone wearing flare. It's not because I want to be rude to the staff—as a former server myself, I know they don't want to sing, and I simply cannot bear *that* kind of attention. A flick usually follows the meal. There is always at least one decent or fun-bad movie released during that first week of October or late September. Typically it's one of those films that's five stars and also just one star. You know, fun-bad. It all adds up to the perfect amount of birthday activity. Anything less than that and friends/coworkers will make me feel bad the next day when they ask me what I did for my birthday. If I say I did nothing, they will look down on me, sinking the emotional ship even further. Anything more outlandish and those same people will not only make me feel bad for not including them, but they will also judge me for doing too much. Suddenly you're one of those attention-seeking crazies in their eyes.

Detour

Another birthday tradition is watching my favorite episode of *Sex and the City*. It's season four, episode one, titled "The Agony and the Extacy." The episode centers around Carrie's thirty-fifth birthday, but it has a little bit of everything. There's Samantha's sexual obsession with her priest ("Friar Fuck"), Charlotte's frustration with Trey's sex drive, and a birthday party from hell. It all culminates in the women meeting for some late-night food, Carrie in tears, monologuing to the girls about being thirty-five and alone, only to end with Charlotte suggesting they all be each other's soulmates instead of looking at men to fill the position. It's a beautiful moment and, to me, the crux of the entire series in that one scene at the end. Carrie leaves the restaurant and Big is waiting outside her apartment with balloons. It's sad but hopeful.

Not sure how this got so bleak, but another thing I hate is opening gifts in front of people. The pressure to perform as the person who was gifted an item is far greater than the pressure to perform in the bedroom or work, or anywhere else, really. There's nothing worse than having all eyes on you, waiting to see how much you like a gift. You're forced to show the right mix of excitement, gratitude, and emotion, and it never feels like enough. When I open gifts, I barely have time to notice the actual item because I'm so worried about reacting appropriately and reaching the expectations that the other person has set for me. And those cards that have graves on them and tell people they're "over the hill" with a picture of Grim Reaper? Give me one of those if you want our relationship to end. I'd rather get a hug from Satan himself than a piece of paper from a friend telling me that I'm close to death. All of this is to say that I'm an impossible nightmare on my birthday.

THIS IS MEAN, NOT CUTE

One October a few years ago, the Lady Gaga *A Star Is Born* remake was released, so of course, it became my birthday movie. Not quite the good-bad style film I usually see, but I was excited because it's Queen Gaga and the reviews were great. I told my boyfriend I wanted to see it on a Saturday afternoon at my favorite movie theater in Los Angeles. This theater has plush reclining chairs, cozy (clean) blankets, and servers that bring you food and drinks throughout the flick. Tickets are a little pricey, but it's justifiable for a special occasion.

"Do you want to invite any friends?" my boyfriend asked when he was preordering the tickets the week prior.

"I don't know, surprise me," I said, with my Libra-ness on full display, uninterested in making a concrete decision.

When it was finally time, we got in the car and headed to the theater. A lot of my close friends were suspiciously quiet leading up to my big day, so I thought maybe they were planning a surprise or that my boyfriend planned something, but I couldn't be sure.

Normally we would get to the theater early to have a drink and order some food before the previews started, but we ran into some traffic and arrived after the lights had already gone down. We sat in our seats, cozied up with the provided blanket, and basked in the glory of a Jennifer Lopez movie trailer. I always enter a trance when I'm in a darkened movie theater, my favorite place on earth.

The feature presentation started, and I got lost in Lady Gaga's performance and Bradley Cooper's mumble mouth. He spent the entire film talking like he had a yapper full of marbles or a spoonful of peanut butter, so it felt like I had to pay extra attention to understand what was going on. I was on the edge of my seat.

About midway through, I noticed a man in front of me stand up and head out to what I assumed was the bathroom. The light from the screen caught the corner of his face for a split second, and as he turned around, I realized he was familiar. It was Jonathan Groff...I think.

For the unfamiliar, Jonathan Groff is an actor who starred in HBO's *Looking* and *Glee* and played Kristoff in the *Frozen* movies. He's also Lea Michelle's best friend. Lea Michelle, of course, starred in *Glee*, and at the time of this movie-going experience, there were no widely available allegations against her. I only knew her as the lead of a show I liked and one of the eighty-seven celebrities in Garry Marshall's *New Year's Eve*, so my excitement was through the roof!

When I realized it might be Jonathan Groff, I looked down at the person seated next to him. It was *the* Lea Michelle...I think. As a certified Gleek who watched every episode of that series from 2009–2015, I was excited. Again, remember that was a different time and *Glee* was popular! STOP JUDGING ME! HINDSIGHT IS TWENTY-TWENTY!! A LOT OF US LIKED IT!!! My boyfriend knew how much I liked the show, and that sent my inner dialog into overdrive.

"Did my boyfriend plan for Lea Michelle and J. Groff to be here? Is Lea going to sing 'Happy Birthday' to me after the movie? Who else is in the audience?! I hope Matthew Morrison doesn't pop out," I thought.

I started to look to see who else was around me. The seats are so far apart in those rooms with the reclining chairs that it was hard to tell, but I thought I maybe saw my friend Nick. And perhaps across the way was my buddy Amy. And in the back it's possible I noticed one of my besties Jenna. I looked over at my man and he was already fast asleep, snoring while Gaga was singing "Shallow." How could he fall asleep during such an iconic movie performance? I figured the only logical reason was that he was taking a nap because he knew as soon as the credits rolled that he would have to get the party started and present a Lea Michelle/Jonathan Groff duet in front of a room full of my friends. HE PLANNED TO HAVE THEM SING TO ME ON MY BIRTHDAY...right?!

The rest of the film was a blur. Aside from looking around the theater and trying to figure out who was there, I was mesmerized by Maybe Lea Michelle watching Lady Gaga's feature film debut. I thought about how it must've killed Lea that it wasn't her on that screen. Surely the role was something she wanted, because what singing young actress wouldn't? Plus, she's a notable Barbra Streisand fan, and A Star Is Born is one of Barbra's most iconic films. On top of all of that, there's the nose subplot. On Glee, they wrote in that Lea's character was considering a nose job. It was the episode they mashed up "I Feel Pretty" with "Unpretty" by TLC, which even typing that sentence proves that show was truly crazed, but I digress. I tried my best to get a clear view of Maybe Lea's face watching Lady Gaga's character, Ally, talk about her sniffer, and it was thrilling.

When I wasn't doing that, I was thinking about what a great boyfriend I had. He organized this all for me, and surely I'd have to repay him on his next birthday, but until then, how could I show my proper gratitude? Like I said, I hate opening gifts and feeling like I have to perform my thankfulness, but this was extra special, and I was willing to do my own best reacting. I HAD to step it up and really lay it on thick when the lights came up in the darkened room. In my seat I practiced my surprise face, warming it up the way a basketball player stretches before a big game. I loosened my jaw and quietly raised my brows, rehearsing what I would do when Lea and Jonathan took to the mic.

At the end of A Star Is Born, Gaga's Ally sings "I'll Never Love Again," a beautiful ballad dedicated to the love of her life, who harrowingly peed himself earlier in the film. In my opinion, it's the best song in it. I think I like it because it feels like a classically '90s movie ballad. "Shallow" is amazing too, don't get me wrong, but that final song breaks me every time I hear it. So, at the end of the movie, Lady Gaga is singing this heart-wrenching ballad, and you can hear the sniffles from everyone in the audience. Well, almost everyone.

In those fancy theaters, the servers come around and bring you your check as the movies are wrapping up. They're shining tiny flashlights on receipts so people pay up before leaving. It's very distracting, especially when a movie is ending as emotionally as *A Star Is Born*. The servers were going to each guest and collecting credit cards from people sobbing from this incredibly sad movie moment, and you can hear the employees being as respectful as possible every time they interrupt someone to get them to pay, but it's frustrating nonetheless. When the server arrived at our area, we weren't exactly crying—my boyfriend was still snoring and I was smiling, practicing my surprised faces, and looking like Taylor Swift winning an award circa 2008.

Eventually the credits began to roll, and the other patrons, including Maybe Jonathan and Maybe Lea, got up to head toward the exit. I assumed they had to go warm up their vocals for my personalized "Happy Birthday" performance. I would've immediately woken up my boyfriend, but I started to think maybe this was all part of his plan. He was pretending to sleep so the theater could clear out and Lea could enter with my besties and "surprise" me. How cute of him.

The credits came to an end, and pretty soon we were the only ones left in the room, outside of a wheelchair user who was waiting for everyone else to clear. There was a split second I thought it might be the Artie character from *Glee*, but alas it was not. My excitement started dwindling when our server came and asked me if there was a problem.

"No, sorry, I was just letting him sleep a little longer," I said, winking when I delivered the word *sleep*.

"Okay, well if you wouldn't mind, we need to clean up for the next showing," the employee replied.

My brain couldn't compute that my fantasy was not going to be a reality. I nudged my boyfriend, and he woke up confused as to why we were sitting in an empty theater with the lights on.

"How long have I been asleep?" he asked.

It finally dawned on me that he wasn't pretending. Slowly but surely, I was starting to get it. We got up and I silently processed the info that Lea and Jonathan wouldn't be serenading me as I ushered in a new year of my life. Before I could accept my fate, my boyfriend told me to wait a minute and that he would be right back.

"I'm so stupid, of course we had to clear the theater, but this surprise is still happening. We just need to go to a different location at the theater, someplace where balloons and banners are already set up, and when I enter, everyone will yell *surprise* and then Lea and Jonathan will be singing to me," I thought to myself as he ran off toward the restroom.

I began to practice my surprise face...again. This time more emotionally spent, so my smile looked like lipstick-smeared Dorinda Medley in Cartagena on *The Real Housewives of New York*.

"What the hell are you doing with your face?" my boyfriend said when he arrived back from the bathroom.

"Oh, nothing, you!" I replied playfully.

"I need to validate. Do you have the parking ticket?" he asked.

I handed it to him, and he slid it into the machine in the lobby to pay.

Instead of leading me into another room in the theater, he began to head outside the building and to the parking garage.

When we got in the car, my excitement once again started to diminish. I thought maybe we were driving to a restaurant or somewhere else for the surprise, but when we pulled down our street, I knew this was it. I didn't say much to him on that drive, and I even started to resent him...

How could he do this to me? How could he not plan to have all my friends see *A Star Is Born* with us and then organize a recording artist and animated film star to sing to me for my birthday?

Unfortunately, I knew I couldn't even hold it against him. It was me who created this fantasy world in my head. I could only be mad at myself, so I would have to let it go, much like Jonathan's *Frozen* costar once sang in what was surely another performance that Lea wished she had booked.

That's the problem with birthdays. There's too much pressure to do something big and too much disappointment if you do something small. Like Goldilocks, I'm forever trying to fill the day with something just right. Like Gaga sang in "Shallow," I, too, am tired of trying to fill that void.

Now that I think about it, perhaps "Shallow" really is the better song.

Lying on the Couch

"You see how picky I am about my
shoes, and they only go on my feet."

CLUELESS (1995)

With the rise of social media, it feels like it's easy to see what tax bracket the people you follow are living in, and it's upsetting to me when the twentysomething influencers are driving expensive cars and living in high-rise city apartments. Am I jealous? Unclear. I have come to learn that, many times, people are bamboozling their followers into thinking they are wealthier than they are, showing off designer brands while living way above their means, so it's hard to tell exactly what's going on inside their purse. Regardless, my twenties were all about saving and scraping by with the bare minimum. In college, my friends and I would save up to go to a buffet that was $3.75 for a huge dinner plate of food every Thursday. On more than one occasion, we would order our meals, sit down, and find a stray quarter in our lo mein. It happened more than once, and we still kept going because it was so cheap and filled our bellies for the day. So many students on campus would pay the $3.75 in all quarters that the establishment had loose change everywhere, including their food. I ate about $1.75 in quarters throughout my time on campus.

In my early twenties, I moved out of the dorms and into a condo with my older brother Bryan. He had a steady income, and the place was big, with an empty loft, so he was kind enough to let me live there for free while I went to school and interned at a Cleveland morning talk show—where I was hired to get coffee for guests like Uncle Joey from *Full House* and a funeral home director who paid to come on the show once a month. The hosts of the show would be cooking with a local restaurateur to open the show, and then after commercial, they would sit down with someone to talk about cremation in a sponsored segment. I loved it. Anyway, although I was working my ass off, none of it was paid, so I couldn't afford things like furniture. My brother let me crash, and my parents had an old bed for me, but there was a large space in the loft that needed a couch and some tables.

After moving in my stuff, my mom saw how empty the space was and offered to take me to look for couches. First up was the garage sale circuit, where we couldn't find anything. Garage sale-ing in Ohio is a sport and the season ends around August, so we were at the tail end, and nothing good was left. Next up we went to the budget stores. We walked into Big Lots and immediately went to their furniture department, which was limited in its selection but did have a pleather sofa for two hundred dollars. When I say pleather, I mean it was some slippery shit. Like a fresh trout, no matter what you were wearing, you would immediately slide off it as soon as you sat down. I think back to my youth when kids would have birthday parties at places like DZ Discovery Zone, where I would try to make it down that roller slide, injuring my butt along the way or getting my oversize hip-hop *Bugs Bunny* shirt caught in the wheels. No one ever slid easily. If the owners of that place really wanted children to move, they should've made a slide that was just one giant pleather couch from Big Lots. Even though the couch was cheap, I didn't care, and to be honest, I didn't even understand at the time what the difference was between real leather and whatever this was. My taste wasn't as refined as it is now. Still, I wanted it and it cost $200, which was the absolute max I had to spend, so the employees wrapped the piece in plastic, and we put it on our truck bed to head home.

Back at the condo, we drove in and noticed my oldest brother, Junior, was parked in the driveway. Junior is like a straight, Italian version of Christopher Lowell. He has impeccable design style, and he's a decisive Taurus, which is helpful to my Libra-ness, so I've come to rely on him for decorating tips. When he saw that I had purchased something, he immediately unwrapped the cheap, black couch to survey our choice.

"You can't keep this," he said without missing a beat.

"It's fine for him," Mom countered.

"It looks like shit and it's pleather."

"He isn't made of money, it's fine."

Mom and Junior argued in front of me about how shitty the couch was that I just spent all my savings to purchase. It was as if I weren't even there.

"He's better off having nothing than this. It's a waste of two hundred dollars!" Junior said.

I started to see that maybe this was not the right fit for my very first non-parent/non-dorm living space. Junior was right, and now I was not only regretful about the ugly-ass sofa, but I was also devastated that I wasted all the money I had on something widely regarded as hideous upon seeing it for the first time. Even my mom admitted it was crap and that she was just being nice when I opted to buy it.

"C'mon, get back in the truck. I'll drive you and we'll return this piece of shit," Junior said.

Without even unloading it into the loft, I got in the car and we made our way back to the store. He is a much faster driver than my mother, so we made it there in record time. However, I did notice when we were on the freeway that a lot of people were honking at us, but I chalked it up to his speed.

Junior pulled into the front of the store, and I ran inside while he waited in the truck. There was no reason for him to go in with me because I knew I would have to first talk to the cashier and convince them that it was an acceptable return.

"I'd like to return a couch I just I purchased," I said to the young employee.

"What's the reason for return?" she asked.

"I literally just got it about an hour ago. Made a mistake," I said.

"Okay, pull around to the back dock. I'll meet you there with the return slip you'll have to sign," she instructed.

We pulled around, backing the truck up to the furniture dock. I hopped out and opened the truck bed just as the employee was coming outside and another was waiting with her. Junior put the truck in park, and he got out to help me unload it.

The four of us looked at the couch at the exact same time, but my brother and I noticed something a split second before the employees. The cushions were no longer on the couch. It seems we may not have properly wrapped the return after all, and the people honking at us on the freeway were doing so because giant pleather cushions were falling one by one out of the back of our truck bed as my brother drove with the fervor of my old friend Roberta on her disability scooter to the discount furniture store.

My mind was racing. There was no way we could retrieve three cushions from a busy Cleveland highway, but I also couldn't afford to be out of the $200 it cost to buy this piece of junk. I had to think fast.

"There are no cushions on this thing," the employee said.

"I KNOW! None," I replied, confirming.

"What happened to them?"

"It didn't come with any," I lied.

"What?" she asked.

"None. No cushions on the couch. That's why I'm returning it."

"But—"

"I can't have a couch with no cushions!"

"You just told me in the store that it was purchased by mistake," she said.

"Right, I forgot to mention that it was sold to me without any cushions. I would've never bought it if I knew."

Junior's face turned bright red, and I could see him biting the inside of his mouth to prevent laughter. I get that he thought it was funny, but

I couldn't afford to screw this up. I shot him a look that said, "Get in the car and pull it together," so he went back into the driver's seat and let me handle the store employees.

"So you want to help me pull this thing out?" I asked the employees.

They were flabbergasted. I assume no one had ever tried to return a sofa before this way, and although I was lying, it seemed like such a far-fetched lie that it had to be true. We unloaded it while my brother sat in the car and giggled like a schoolgirl.

After it was unloaded, the only thing left to do was sign my return slip for the money to be refunded back onto my credit card and scurry out of there as fast as possible. Signing my name never felt so nefarious. I was a fraud. An outlaw. Looking back, I very much regret doing what I did. It's one of only two regrets I have in life, the other being my freshman year of college when I wore a cell phone belt clip. No wonder I wasn't having sex in college—my cell was on display and protruding out of my waistline, but that's a tale for another time. It was completely inappropriate of me to lie and bamboozle this store out of two hundred dollars, and I knew they wouldn't be able to resell it in the shape it was in. Who is going to buy a couch with no cushions? Even so, I signed and got the hell out of there as quickly as possible.

"Thanks so much! Hope you find the cushions," I said to the employees as I got into the passenger's seat of the now-empty truck.

"Go, GO, GO!" I told my brother as if he were a getaway car and I just robbed a bank.

We drove back to the condo, and the whole way, I looked out the window for those cushions, eventually seeing them in the middle of the busiest section of the freeway. For a moment, we considered stopping on the side of the road to pick them up, bring them back to the store, and confess my sins. It would've been incredibly dangerous but perhaps still doable. Instead, we kept driving and I waited on the edge of my seat for the refund to officially post to my account, worrying that they would change their minds and call to tell me to come collect the cushionless furniture. Years later, when I was more grown and financially stable, I would decide to start donating to the Brain and Behavioral Foundation, a fantastic mental health charity. One particular year, I made a donation on behalf of that store as a way to repent. I figured it was the least I could do, and while it might not have been as appropriate as paying them back the two hundred dollars, it felt like a start. Donating to an organization that does brain research felt like the next best thing, since I mindfucked them so hard.

Does the Ring Mean a Thing?

"That's your problem! You don't want to be
in love. You want to be in love in a movie."

SLEEPLESS IN SEATTLE (1993)

On Friday, June 26, 2015, the Supreme Court ruled to make same-sex marriage legal in the United States, effectively opening a whole new world of possibilities for those of us in gay relationships. I turned thirty shortly thereafter. I'm young enough that I was confident gay marriage would be legal in my lifetime, but the reality came speeding toward me like a freight train in 2015.

My boyfriend and I had spent five years together at that point, give or take some tiny breaks where I would dramatically break up with him and spend a couple of days listening to Adele and texting other men before I would come back to my senses. We also broke up once after seeing the movie *Blue Valentine* simply because the movie was so intense and made me feel like true love was impossible, or maybe it was because I thought I would eventually run off with Ryan Gosling,

WE'RE NOT SURE. Despite the drama, I knew my boyfriend and I would eventually end up together. He's not perfect—he wears hats to special occasions, he has more collectibles than my three-year-old niece, and he's #TeamJolie/#TeamKristin (I'll always be #TeamAniston/#TeamLC). That said, he's also super smart, he continues to surprise me, he gets along with my family, and he'll listen to me talk about Katherine Heigl's old ZzzQuil commercials every time I bring it up (approximately biweekly). If you want a lifelong partner, he's the one you want by your side.

So, now that I knew I wanted to marry him and marriage was legal, I just had to figure out the next step. Easy, right? Not for me. Marriage is an institution that's been around forever, and because of that, there are traditions that make little to no sense when applied to me as a homosexual. These traditions sent me into a spiral that had me questioning whether or not I even wanted to get married or if I even believed in marriage. Sure, I fought for the right for same-sex marriage, but that had more to do with equality than it did for my personal need to walk down an aisle. We are so conditioned to think that marriage equals aisle, when in reality, it doesn't have to.

Which brings me to the ring situation. I started to confide in a few close friends that I was going to ask this man to marry me. Everyone had opinions about who should ask whom, but I always knew it would be me asking him, so I just had to get a band. But wait, men don't traditionally wear engagement rings. Heterosexual men usually get one for the woman to wear during the engagement period, and then they get new rings when they actually get married. It's tradition! This is where I started to question the whole institution. Why do women need two rings to symbolize their love? Why don't men need any? I did what any normal person would: I put on an episode of *Vanderpump Rules* and worked in a conversation about engagement rings while we were watching. We decided it would be weird for one person to wear an engagement ring and the other not to wear one, so that issue was settled.

Now that I knew he didn't want an engagement ring, what was I going to do? If you don't have a ring to propose with, then the moment seems unofficial. I started telling my close friends that, and each time I did, it felt like I was letting them down. I could feel the judgment. They would respond with, "I guess that makes sense, but what will you do?" Everyone in my life equated proposing with an actual ring, and there was no changing them. My head became littered with their judgments, and soon my decision-making skills were compromised. I started to think I *needed* a ring. Because I was compromising my own beliefs to please others, I became confused. I also worried that anything short of fulfilling the promise of an engagement would look like a flaw in our relationship, and I didn't want other people to think that. I knew that would lead to friends and family writing off our love, dropping hints to move on, and introducing me to potential new suitors. I internally compromised, concluding that I would get a ring to symbolize the moment, but neither of us would be compelled to actually wear the rings after the asking.

I put on another episode of *Vanderpump Rules* and shopped online. Turns out you can buy rings to be delivered right to your door, and they are perfectly nice and come with a wonderful return policy. Since I feel cheap even typing that sentence, please remember that I was looking for a diamond-less male ring simply to symbolize a proposal and not to actually wear. I shopped as I watched the two Toms, and I ended up buying a black tungsten band that seemed alternative enough for my boyfriend (who is looks-wise described as "creatively tattooed" by my mother) and simple enough for the traditional proposal. I ordered two, convincing myself that I should have a couple different size options, but I realize now I only bought two so we could have the option of Instagramming both of our hands with rings on them (we live in a sick time).

The rings arrived in a couple days, and now I just needed the perfect moment that would impress the people rooting for us. His birthday was coming up and we had a trip to Mexico planned with some friends, so it seemed like the perfect opportunity. The closer we got to the vacation, the more excited I felt. I stopped worrying about the politics of rings and marriage and felt ready to commit my life to one man. I even had time to plan personal touches without the influence of others in my head. He likes Legos, so I had some little Lego guys made to look like us, complete with cute little Lego tuxes. The plan was to give the Lego men to him and then when he questioned why they were in tuxes, I could present the ring and say, "Will you marry me?" I didn't have the other details or words planned out, but I knew they would come to me when we got to Mexico.

His birthday week finally arrived, and we packed for our Cabo San Lucas getaway. I've never been to Mexico, but I assumed it would be exactly like the *Sex and the City* movie where the girls take Carrie's honeymoon trip after Big fails to show up on time to the altar. Perhaps it was because I associated Mexico with Carrie drama, but as soon as we landed, I started to feel internally crazy and things took a dark turn for me emotionally. All those people I told about our special moment were texting or calling to find out the details, asking me when I was going to ask him to marry me. All the pressure froze me and caused me to panic. I was putting on a brave face, but inside I felt like Carrie when she couldn't eat anything and Samantha has to come in and feed her pudding. I wished I had someone to feed me pudding, because instead I ate ALL the food at the all-inclusive resort, which led to a stomach parasite. So romantic. Regardless, I called my mom for some guidance.

Mom tried to calm me down, and in between trips to the bathroom, I did my best to psych myself up for the proposal. Lots of other friends were calling and texting, asking me how it was going to go. I couldn't back out now, but I did finally snap. In the words of the poster for *Snapped*, an Oxygen series, "Everyone has a breaking point." I texted all my people to stop asking me anything about the engagement, and I retreated to my hotel room.

The next day was his actual birthday, and we had group dinner plans. Everyone was expecting me to quiet the room and get down on one knee at the restaurant, but I refused. Instead, just the two of us went back to the room after dinner and stripped down to our more comfortable outfits (oversize house shirts and underwear). Without anyone else around, I went to the bathroom one last time—a mix of nerves and that nasty stomach parasite.

When I went back into the main room, I saw my boyfriend lying in the hotel bed, playing a word game on his iPad, and everything became clear again. It was just him and me, alone, and a sense of calm came over me. The nerves were still there but buried a little deeper.

Stronger than that though, was the assuredness that his love would make everything okay. In that moment, I felt like I could lose everything else—my home, my money, my stuff. It wouldn't matter as long as I didn't lose him. I told him to close his eyes, and I put the little Lego guys in his hands. He opened his eyes and smiled. For a few seconds, his lips curled upward, he flashed his beautiful teeth, and inspected the two of us in Lego form. Like a child, he played with them as if they really were me and him. Just like my niece would do, he put the little arms together and made them kiss. I hadn't even asked him to marry me yet, but in that moment, he said yes. It was in his eyes that he wanted to be with me forever, and the fact that I wanted to be with him forever was radiating from my own. None of that other stuff mattered. That was the moment *for us* when we got engaged. I followed by getting on one knee and pulling out the ring I bought online. I asked him, he said yes. That was the moment for everyone else. The ring part of the story was enough to please our friends and family when we went back to tell them, but the moment before was enough to please me when I look into his eyes again in twenty or thirty or forty years.

The entire experience made me realize that love, marriage, and tradition are meant to bend, to be flexible. You can't propose for other people or fall in love in the way you see in the movies. After I saw the warmth in his eyes, I made a conscious effort to strive to do everything in our own way. Instead of rushing to call or tell other people, we celebrated the way we wanted. We lay in that Mexican hotel bed, ordered room service, and watched HBO's *The Comeback* (which is the greatest TV show ever) on an iPad. I put my head on his chest, relieved that nothing changed. We eventually got around to posting an update online and calling our friends and family. Their love and support was appreciated, but it didn't mean as much to me as it did before. We have no plans to get married at the moment, but we do have a commitment that we understand and that I'm glad I made. It turns out the ring didn't mean a thing after all.

Detour

A good loved one is always just a phone call away.

Phone calls with Mom are usually me ringing her when I lose a job opportunity, or when my boyfriend and I get in a fight. Really any big life moment. Half the time she'll answer her cell from the grocery store or a TJ Maxx, because she, too, is a certified Maxxinista. Like clock-work, she gets distracted by the world around her, even if she answers my call from her own home.

"Hello?" she'll say as she picks up my call.

"Hi, Ma! My anxiety is really bad right now, I'm not sure what I should do about—"

"Hold on, Dan, that bold-ass woodpecker is back at the window. (Yelling to my father) Gary! The bold-ass woodpecker is back at the window!"

Here I was thinking she would simply pause the competition for the Mirrorball trophy that she was watching and focus on me.

"Is now a bad time, Ma?"

"No, I can talk, but this bold-ass woodpecker is driving me nuts! It pecks at the window...(imitating) ba-ba-ba-ba-ba! I can't hear it anymore, I'm sick of it. But I'm good now, what do you need?"

"It's the ring, I—"

"Hold on, Dan, your Aunt Joanne is calling on the house phone."

"(To Joanne) Jo, yeah, I can't talk long, Dan's on the other phone, but you'll never guess who's back...the bold-ass woodpecker! I'm gonna have to start chargin' it rent! Ya know what, I'm gonna have to call you back, Jo, Dan's on the other line."

"(To me) Dan, sorry, that was your Aunt Joanne, had to tell her about the woodpecker. These critters are gonna have to start paying the mortgage! We got a deck squirrel, a slinky cat that's been coming around. Your Aunt Joanne's got a smiley raccoon that's always smiling! You know what it's smiling about? It gets to live rent free!" she says then turns her attention to my father.

"(To Dad) Gary, go spray the window with Windex to get it out of here, or at least ask it for a rent check because it acts like it owns the joint!"

"(To me) You know, Debbie next door feeds the critters. She's got the bird feeder and I saw her put out a plate of food! Leftovers! And they still come to my yard, not hers. Imagine if I started feeding the critters here, it'd be a zoo! I'd have a Noah's ark if I put out my world-famous potato salad. Anyway, what does my Danster need?" she finally asks.

"It's—"

"Hold on, Dan!"

"(To Dad) Gary, you're at the wrong window!" she shouts at my father through the glass.

"(To me) Your father is at the wrong window. I gotta go out there and tell him. I mean, he's cleaning the window, at least I finally got him doing that, but I need that bold-ass woodpecker gone. They don't like the smell of the Windex, so it goes away when you spray around it. Ya know what, I better go, congrats, or hope everything's okay. Love ya!" she says, hanging up on me and leaving me with no choice but to smile.

As I get older, I see that we're all in our own little worlds, dealing with not just the big life events, but also the minutia of an everyday existence. Our friends and family may want us to give them their undivided attention, but it's not always possible. As life gets busier and busier, I'm grateful to have people in my life who will answer no matter what the circumstance. I count myself lucky to know that I have even just a handful of family and friends I can call in the middle of the night, the break of dawn, or when a bold-ass woodpecker is at their window.

Wedding Exercise

"I go online, and my breath catches in my chest
until I hear three little words: You've got mail."

YOU'VE GOT MAIL (1998)

Weddings bring out the absolute worst in people. It's supposed to be a time of love, celebration, and gathering with the people closest to you, but really it is a time when humans become the most berserk, selfish version of themselves all the while wearing rented clothes and dancing to "Shout." By the end of the reception, someone's Uncle Larry is shouting at you because his table was placed right next to a speaker that ruined his already-bad hearing. You're trying to pat your pits dry while Uncle Larry's inability to "get a little bit softer now" has you checking for the shuttle bus back to the hotel. While the ceremony and reception is a lot to handle, it's the buildup to the special day that has me questioning humanity. If you've ever been part of a wedding party, specifically the bridal side, you know what I'm talking about.

I've had the (mis)fortune of being a part of four weddings during my short time here on earth. The first came when I was eighteen and brother number one was tying the knot. I shared best man duties, and my only real responsibility was showing up to the bachelor party, which consisted of a weekend in Vegas with the other groomsmen and the bridal party, as well as a woman nicknamed Gina Rails, whom I'm still not certain had any connection to the group. She received her moniker by taking her first name and putting it in front of the word *rails*, because she was known for proudly doing rails of cocaine at any given moment. Seeing a young woman on coke at a Vegas breakfast brunch buffet was a lot for my teenage eyes to handle. I'll never forget "Killing Me Softly" playing over the loudspeaker and her shouting along while we were in line for heat-lamped scrambled eggs. An older gentleman was behind me and simply said, "She's killing me loudly with that voice," as he reached for a sausage link using the pancake tongs. An icon.

Brother number two's wedding also found me in the best man position. This time I was in my midtwenties, and instead of a bachelor party weekend, we opted for one night out in downtown Cleveland. It wasn't just the groomsmen who joined this party—it was also my dad and uncles, all of whom are married already, celebrating together at a strip club. Married people, in my experience, act one of two ways at a strip club. They either get WAY too into the dancers, dropping all their money in hopes that one of the women will magically decide to leave with them and start a new life, or the married guys awkwardly fumble around, doing their best to prove they have zero interest in the bubbies around them. For this occasion, we got a VIP table and a bunch of booze, and at this establishment, the dancers come to the VIP to try to coerce the men into getting a private dance, where they in turn earn more money. One of the gals asked my dad for a private show, and he falls into the awkward category. You see, Dad had become newly obsessed with his Nike FuelBand, which were all the rage at the time, so when the woman was flirtatiously questioning him about a special dance, he was checking his steps and telling her how his new gadget works. Their convo went something like this:

"Hi stud, do you want a private dance?"

"I'm kind of busy right now checking my fuel points. I did a long walk earlier, but I still need a few more steps. Might have to take a lap around this place. Do you know the circumference? Ya know what, don't worry about it, I can measure it on my app. Why don't you go ahead and ask one of these other guys."

It's a good thing he met my mother in the 1970s.

The young lady moved on to me, and I quickly told the stripper that although I respect her craft, the only sexual dancing I'm interested in seeing up close is the "I'm a Slave For U" choreography from Britney's self-titled album (would've also settled for something from the *Oops! I Did It Again* era).

This one, singular night out was pretty much all I had to do for brother number two's wedding. There was very little preplanning, no decorations or group texts. However, I came to find out a few years later that being in a bridal party is *much* different than being a groomsman. Bridal parties are fully deranged.

First of all, I don't believe anyone wants to be in a bridal party. If you're out there and you're getting married or in the process of getting married, you can pretend your friends and family want to be in your wedding, but I'm here to tell you that they don't. There are exceptions to every rule, of course, but you brides make your friends go through too many hoops in addition to just the bachelorette party. Plus, the bachelorette party is VERY different than a bachelor party. Straight men are happy to simply see some bare breasts and have a beer. Hell, gay men just need a male stripper dancing to "Pony" or Christina Aguilera's "Dirrty" to be satisfied. But straight women require games, decorations, and hundreds of dollars of dick merch (dick straws, dick lollipops, dick balloons, dick-cetera...) before they're ready to move on to the ceremony. It should be noted that it's not just the bride who is troublesome; the entire group ends up being a mess. There's always at least one person in the bridal party who is going to be the puker. They drink too much and throw up at every single wedding event. I'm talking vomit with the strippers, vomit at the engagement party, vomit at the rehearsal dinner. They're the ones who refuse to eat on the wedding day and force the limo/party bus to pull over so they can upchuck on the way to the church. You offer them a handful of pretzels and a couple almonds, but they decline, only to hurl an inexplicable amount of champagne out the side of a limousine. Whenever a bride is late, I don't even consider cold feet, I always just assume it's because a girl named Brooke didn't space out her champs and is making everyone wait for her to clean the sick off her dress with an old Tide pen someone tossed in their purse before leaving the hotel that morning.

In addition, the bridal party stuff is all SO expensive. I think parties are great, but weddings have gotten out of hand and the entire industry needs to be stopped. ENOUGH.

A couple years back, wedding number four was up and running: a friend was getting hitched and graciously asked me to be her "Man of Honor." She is one of my all-time favorite people, and if it were literally anyone else, I would've said no, but I put on a smile and agreed to handle my business as a bestie because I love her more than almost anyone on the entire planet. While I had been in weddings before, this was my first time in the number one position on the bride side, so I had a lot to learn. The bride's sister was kind enough to help with the organizing and other responsibilities, so together we planned a bachelorette weekend in New Orleans, and I ordered my outfit for the wedding photos. A couple weeks before we were all set to go to NOLA to celebrate, the pandemic hit. All the dick merch I bought was nonrefundable, but there were more important things happening in the world to worry about.

With the deadly pandemic in full effect, I expected no one in the wedding party to be concerned with the canceled bachelorette weekend, but I WAS WRONG. Emails continued to flood in those early days as no one was certain just how long life would be on lockdown. My boyfriend lost his job, I lost a lot of my work, just as many others around the world did, but the emails about wedding activities continued through it all. I didn't even know if we would all safely make it out of 2020, so the last thing on my mind was wedding stuff.

The day my boyfriend lost his paycheck was the same day I lost one of my main paid gigs for the year. At night, an email came in from Patricia, one of the women from the bridal party, suggesting that we do something special for the bride and groom in lieu of the canceled weekend of bridal party fun in Louisiana.

"I hate that we are going to have to reschedule the bachelorette party! We should do something to cheer them up," she wrote.

That's a beautiful idea in theory, but remember I am broke at this point and barely hanging on to my sanity. I was locked in a tiny apartment with my unemployed significant other, binging *RuPaul's Drag Race* as my hair grew to unspeakable lengths and I obsessively washed my hands every five seconds, wondering when I'd ever get to see my family again. I had an empty bank account and I WAS ON THE EDGE.

As I continued reading the email, I expected to see the suggestion of sending a nice card or a small floral arrangement, but instead Patricia suggested that we all buy the bride and groom a Peloton. A PELOTON BIKE! Don't get me wrong, I LOVE those fancy exercise bikes with the screens attached, and as far as I'm concerned, instructor Cody Rigsby is a national hero, but these pieces of equipment are P-R-I-C-E-Y, and this woman was not suggesting we pitch in and get it *in place of* a wedding gift. No, no, we were still expected to do a bachelorette weekend once the country opened up, as well as the engagement gift, wedding gift, tux rental, etc. And don't forget all those nonrefundable schlong straws. Peloton Patty was simply suggesting it as *an additional* gift, since the bride was inconvenienced in having to postpone the pre-party/ bachelorette weekend because of the deadly pandemic that at this point had changed the course of history as we knew it. All the emotion I had been burying deep regarding the state of the world, the sadness of not being able to see my family, wondering how I was going to pay rent, and the uncertainty of our nation's future came bubbling up to the surface as I read that message asking me to buy someone a Peloton.

I've never been a confrontational person. Ordinarily, I spend my days thinking about what I wish I would've said to someone who wronged me instead of actually saying any of those things. I win so many of the imaginary fights in my head, but they often stay there.

My brain was in overdrive and my hands were shaking as I clicked the *reply* button. I did my absolute best not to explode my anger onto the screen. I wished I had the strength to respond with exactly how I felt, but I bit my tongue. The email response I typed was polite, stating that I thought it was insensitive to ask me and the other people in the bridal party to chip in to buy a piece of exercise equipment for the bride when so many have lost their jobs and/or are dealing with illness and the general hell of 2020. Very kindly, I suggested that perhaps, maybe if anyone has any extra money, they could donate it to a worthy cause instead of pitching in for an exercise bike. Easy breezy. None of the snappy comebacks playing inside my head made it to the final draft, which I thought was a good thing... I was keeping the peace. Or so I thought. After I clicked send, I got another email, this time from a boss at a writing gig I had been hired for. They informed me that although I had already done a lot of work on the project, they wouldn't be able to pay me. I snapped. I hopped on over to Twitter, where I voiced my actual frustration, like the petty Millennial I am, about the wedding. After all, I couldn't vent about the job drama because I didn't want to burn any professional bridges. Instead, I let my feelings about the exercise bike and the insanity of bridal parties ooze out of me for my entire timeline to ingest. Big mistake. Huge.

"The straights are CRAZY when it comes to weddings! Someone just asked me to buy a Peloton for a bride because the pandemic is causing them to reschedule the bachelorette party," I tweeted. I continued into a thread of details, making sure to not include any specific names but dragging the events nonetheless. It wasn't even the bike so much as all of my feelings being let out at once on something that it made sense for me to be mad about. It's never about what it's about.

The likes on Twitter started coming in fast and furious. Celebrities who follow me on social media were replying things like, "What the hell is wrong with people?" Every time someone hearted my tweets, I felt a validation that I wasn't crazy for thinking it was a weird ask. I felt at peace. Briefly.

Less than five minutes from when I posted, I got a ding on my computer. A new email came in, this time from Peloton Patty's boyfriend.

"Tweeting about my girlfriend is a dick move! She has a real job and all you do is tell jokes for a living," he said.

I felt like Carrie Bradshaw when she got an instant message on her computer in *Sex and the City*. She ducked for cover, worrying that someone could see her. Keep in mind, I had never met either of these people in person, and I had no idea they even followed me on Twitter. I didn't even understand how the boyfriend had my email address. Doesn't matter, they were both pissed.

Before I could even catch my breath, the phone rang. It was the bride.

"Did you tweet something about Patricia asking you to buy a Peloton?" she asked in that shaky voice that makes me nervous.

"What? What are you talking about?" I replied, knowing exactly what she was talking about but trying to buy myself time to assess the severity of the situation. At this point I felt all my bowels lower.

"She's crying right now, so upset. Can you delete the tweets?" she said.

And just like that, I became the doggone villain. A stranger asked me to collect all my coins to buy a bride a Peloton in the midst of the deadliest pandemic since 1918, and I was now feeling bad for saying how I felt to my close friends (Twitter).

I've been known to expunge my tweets a time or two. I consider the ones I anxiously delete within a few minutes of posting to be exclusives that are only available for a limited time. Of course, I ended up deleting these specific wedding tweets, but not because of Peloton Patty—I did it because my best friend asked me to and those are the rules. In the buildup to your friend's wedding, you have to do whatever they want, no matter what.

In retrospect, I should've screenshotted the emails they sent and called them out by name on Twitter. That's what social media is for. You voice your frustrations, which is what I was doing. It's a Burn Book! Not only that, but that the boyfriend was so bossy *and* reduced my profession in saying that all I do is "tell jokes for a living." Why was he even getting involved with bridal party drama? Doesn't he watch *The Real Housewives*? The men should NEVER get in the mix. And why did that couple call the bride and groom about all this nonsense? There was no reason to stress them out, as they already had enough on their plate, what with their postponed wedding and the 2020 trauma we were all collectively going through.

The bride and groom canceled their big plans and instead did a small ceremony at a courthouse, and I never came face to face with my new archnemeses, Peloton Patty or her boyfriend. Part of me was relieved because seeing this couple that I had such a tense and awkward email exchange with would have been more than uncomfortable. The downside was that I didn't get to see my best friend say "I do" to the man she loves. As cynical as I may be about weddings, I love seeing love (fingers crossed they still have a fondness for me after reading this chapter about the events that unfolded via email and social media).

They also ended up buying their own exercise bike in place of a honeymoon, and while I may simply tell jokes for a living, those strangers both followed me on Twitter without ever actually meeting me in person, so they must like at least some of my humor. I like to think that 2020 was making us all crazy and maybe I will someday see Peloton Patty and Bossy Boyfriend and we can laugh the whole experience off over cocktails. After all, how can any of us be held accountable for our words or actions throughout that hellscape? Or maybe they're reading this book and hate me even more for continuing on this saga. Perhaps it all would've all been avoided if I acted more like Berger than I did Carrie in *Sex and the City*, by simply replying to that initial email with, "I'm sorry. I can't. Don't hate me." Or maybe if I would've just changed the subject like my dad did with that beautiful exotic dancer, I could've gone for a walk and got my steps in instead of getting tangled in online drama.

Friday Night Lights

"This is not a democracy, it's a cheerocracy."

BRING IT ON (2000)

Friday night football games are a huge deal when you grow up in Solon, Ohio. Everyone gathers to watch the varsity team play, all the while the cheer team plasters on smiles and waves their pom-poms at everyone sitting on the bleachers. If I close my eyes, I can picture myself as a young kid underneath those bleachers, listening to the feet stomp above me in unison, the smell of cheap nacho cheese in the air, and the crisp, chill sweatshirt weather. I'm not a football fan, but I'd give anything to go back and relive one of those evenings where the only care in the world is whose house you were going to sleep at that night or whether or not you were going to make it to Applebee's after the game to split one order of chicken tenders with eleven other teens.

When I was fifteen, just a couple months into my high school experience, I would drive to the field with my folks, and they would sit with some adult friends, while I would venture off into the student section with the other high school kids. The student area was tiered off so seniors had the best seats, freshmen had the worst, and just about everyone was sneaking beer in water bottles or flasks they hid under blankets. The nights were always about more than sports; they were about the socializing and drama. Games of telephone would echo throughout the stands, with teenage whispers filling the air—who liked whom and who was breaking up with whom. Throughout the week, students would create their story lines between classes, and Friday night football games would be where it all climaxed, where the dirty laundry was aired. I wouldn't say I was a loser by any means, but I was B-list at best, so I mostly observed.

It might be hard to tell, since you're all reading a book about me, but I've never loved attention. It's okay when I have complete control over it, but that's such a rare occurrence, and I particularly loathe it when it comes to anything regarding romance or sexuality. Growing up closeted, I never felt comfortable in my own skin. People often ask me when I knew I was gay, and the truth is, I always kind of knew, but I was raised in a place where there weren't many, if any, LGBTQ+ people around me. Being that there were no real-life examples, I worked hard to convince myself that the inklings I had about being gay weren't real or substantial. To add to that, teenage hormones are so aggressive that it's hard to know what—or who—you like. Did I want to hook up with the other young women in my school, or did I want to play M.A.S.H. and theorize what it was like behind the scenes of the *Vanity Fair* cover shoot that featured the Olsen twins, Hilary Duff, Lindsay Lohan, Raven-Symoné, Mandy Moore, Evan Rachel Wood,

Alexis Bledel, and Amanda Bynes on the cover? It was the latter, but I didn't quite know it yet.

Detour

Remember when *Saved by the Bell* did the Malibu Sands Beach Club episodes? The sight of Zack Morris in a sleeveless neon blouse left me weak at the knees, and when he and Mario Lopez took off their tops to play volleyball? I salivated. But for every time I got twitter-pated by those two, I would also get the feels for Kelly Kapowski or Lisa Turtle in a bathing suit. I was so excited, so scared that I was attracted to everyone, and that confused the crap out of me when it came to my sexuality. Looking back, there were so many seminal moments from both genders that got my heart racing, but it was *mostly* about the men. Here are more than a few that come immediately to mind...

Devon Sawa in *Casper*. He only appeared for a couple of minutes, but seeing his perfect hair slow dance with Christina Ricci to a Jordan Hill ballad was one of the first times I remember being attracted to the same gender. When I saw him pop up in *Now and Then* (underrated) the same year, I was fully crushed, and his role in *Little Giants* made me want to play football, or at least re-watch the football-themed film again and again.

Rebecca Gayheart in *90210*. One of the most beautiful humans ever, and her gorgeous eyes on screen in *90210* confused the hell out of me. I'll never, ever forget when her character...SPOILER ALERT... died. I CRIED SO MUCH THAT NIGHT.

Josh Hartnett! Even though his hair in the '90s made it look like he got in a fight with a Weedwacker, he was still stunning. His neck mole was, and remains, very influential to my development.

Queer as Folk (US). The original UK version is superior, but during my high school years, I discovered the drama on Showtime in the basement of my parents' house after they were asleep. The Brian/Justin romance was my gay lighthouse.

Tyson Beckford. Whew! Five stars. Remember when he did the Toni Braxton video?

The Lawrence Brothers in that Disney Channel Original Movie where they were shipwrecked and blouse-less. In the immortal words of Joey in *Blossom*… "Whoa!"

Denise Richards in *Wild Things*. Before her two-season arc on *The Real Housewives of Beverly Hills*, Denise lit up the screen in some serious classic films. While my favorite movie of hers is *Drop Dead Gorgeous*, it was her tour de force in *Wild Things* that really made me question everything. I truly believe that the hotness of Denise in that film knows no bounds. Bonus points for the Kevin Bacon shower scene at the end.

Tony Danza in *Who's the Boss?*

Kurt Russell as Captain Ron.

Eric Nies from *The Real World*. I actually didn't watch his season of *The Real World* until recently (Heather B. is now my everything), but I remember Eric's abs frequently appearing on MTV during the early '90s and young me being so enamored. Other *Real World* alum who got me going include: Alton from Las Vegas, Colin from Hawaii, and Danny from New Orleans. Speaking of MTV, special shout-out to the spring break coverage, specifically the episode of Jerry Springer that was filmed at a beach and aired on MTV featuring men with whipped-cream bikinis.

Aladdin and Prince Eric from *The Little Mermaid*.

Keanu Reeves in *Speed*, specifically the second half when he's wearing just a white tee, but also every frame of Keanu Reeves in anything.

Michelle Pfeiffer as Catwoman. One of the greatest performances ever, so good that anyone who saw it was attracted to her. The scene where she dances with Michael Keaton in *Batman Returns*...a moment!

Cuba Gooding Jr. when he hosted *SNL* and did a sketch where he stripped for the Mango character.

Various *Mighty Morphin Power Rangers*, specifically Tommy, Jason, and Adam the Black Ranger in the feature film when he was assigned the Frog Zord. Johnny Yong Bosch really awakened something within me in that moment. The Kimberly envy within was also real.

Chris Evans's *Flaunt* magazine photo shoot. Apparently we're unable to reprint the photos in this book, but Google it.

Leonardo DiCaprio in *The Beach*. I rented that movie from my local library upwards of eighty-five times and I can't tell you what it's about, but Leo was tan and rarely wearing a top...five stars!

Tom Welling as Superman.

Janet Jackson in the "If" video.

Ricky Martin with the candle wax in the "Livin' La Vida Loca" video.

The Playgirl paparazzi photos of Brad Pitt from the late '90s (which were allegedly the inspo for Shania Twain singing about him not impressing her much). Brad always impresses me.

Ryan Phillippe. I already mentioned him in this book, but it bears repeating that his butt is one of the most important butts of all time.

Cruel Intentions is the most well-known performance of his butt, but *54* also has an iconic butt shot. Ryan also has a shower scene in IKWYDLS (*I Know What You Did Last Summer*) that, although it doesn't show off his ass-ets, it was very important to me, and leads me to the final piece of my sexual confusion puzzle...

Jennifer Love Hewitt. She was the girl next door and a bombshell, although my crush was completely nonsexual. Unlike the others I mentioned, JLH didn't rev up my sex engine, she just seemed like someone I wanted to marry. I first fell in love with her in *Party of Five*, but my love continued with IKWYDLS and ISKWYDLS (*I Still Know What You Did Last Summer*), her music, and more. I even watched the *Party of Five* spin-off she did with Jennifer Garner (#Justice4TimeOfYourLife) and bought her album (#Justice4BareNaked). The point is, I was in love. Eventually, J. Love would be a guest on my podcast, and interviewing her was a real moment for me. I had her poster on my wall, and she was suddenly in my kitchen, and let me tell you, she was a DELIGHT. I'm not sure if she would even remember me, since celebs do so much press, but she was kind, warm, and even willing to recreate her iconic line, "What are you waiting for?" from IKWYDLS. Blessed.

Anyway, my crush on Jennifer Love Hewitt was real back then, and when I met a girl named Sarah, who looked like the spitting image of her, I was convinced she was going to be the love of my life. The first time I met her was at an open house I went to with my parents. Sarah's family was moving to town and I happened to meet her at the house her family ultimately moved into. My parents loved to go to open houses just for fun, which used to sound boring to me, but now that I'm an adult and spending roughly three hours a night browsing Zillow with a bottle of bed wine, I get it. Just a few short weeks after that meeting, Sarah and I would be going to the same school. I got home that day after the open house, ran up to my bedroom, and listened to Brandy's "Have You Ever" on repeat for about six hours, dreaming of starting my life with her, having kids, and becoming Mr. Sarah, or whatever the proper equivalent of that is.

For the most part, Sarah and I never spoke more than three words to each other. I'd say hi or ask how she was, she would respond, and then I would run away with heart palpitations. Every time we talked, my voice would shake, my eyes would twitch, and I would sweat even more than normal (my body was like a waterfall). She made me incredibly nervous, and saying more than a few words to her was entirely too much for me to handle. Plus, she was one of the most popular kids in school, despite being a new student. She was *that* good looking.

All that's to say that one Friday night, I decided I was going to talk to Sarah and invite her to the fall dance. I'm not sure where I got the nerve to think that she would go with me since she was A-list and I was the kid who listened to a Brandy ballad for six hours straight on more than one occasion, but I digress. Did I mention I also dressed up like the "Have You Ever" music video, using a cherry-flavored Airheads candy to give me a bold lip to recreate Brandy's look? The point is, I was confident and delusional, which is how I would describe most of my youth until this time.

For days leading up to me asking her to the dance, I obsessed over how I would do it and what she might say. I'd role-play, pretending

Sarah was an inflatable green alien that I won at a carnival game, analyzing every possible outcome, planning out what I would wear, and daydreaming about what I would say if she said yes. While I knew there was a possibility that she would turn me down, the reward far outweighed the risk.

School was rough that Friday, since I wasn't able to concentrate on anything other than my weekend plans. My brother and I were the same height, so most of my clothes were his hand-me-downs. Every once in a while, he would let me wear some of his more current stuff, and this particular night, I asked him to help dress me. He gave me something I definitely couldn't pull off, sprayed me with half of a bottle of Nautica cologne, and let me borrow some of his hair gel, which was the kind that turns your hair into a rock. Remember in *Hocus Pocus* when Bette Midler turns to stone as the sun rises? That's basically what happened when I put that gel in my hair. Actually, I *wish* I looked as good as Queen Bette when she was made of stone. I was addicted to acne cream at the time, and my hair was prematurely gray, so the combination of my dry skin and graying hair made me look more like that *Hocus Pocus* zombie who wakes up on Halloween and coughs dust.

Even though my brother helped dress me, he had no plans to go to the football game. He was a freshman in college nearby, so he was way too cool to go to his old high school's game. Instead, I once again drove with my parents, who were excited to hang with some of the other parents under a blanket while watching football.

We arrived at the field and assumed our usual routine; Mom and Dad went to meet their friends while I met mine.

"Meet us down by the concessions at the end of the game," Mom said.

While there WERE cell phones at that time, the Pellegrino family only had one that we all shared. Nowadays, even my eight-year-old niece has a cell, but pre-millennium/pre-*Willennium* (the Will Smith album that featured a song called "Will 2K"), they weren't as common.

For the first half of the football game, I anxiously ran around with my friends, stress-eating concession hot dogs and reconsidering my plans to ask Sarah on a date. During halftime I saw her with her bestie, giggling in my direction, and I worried they were both making fun of me. I was convinced that someone must've told her I was going to ask her to the dance, and now she had plenty of time to plan her way of saying no, along with making fun of me for even *thinking* she would go with me.

You ever hear those stories about people able to lift a car in moments of strength, adrenaline giving them what they need to do impossible tasks? That's what happened to me in the third quarter. Her friend went off to the bathroom or something, and I noticed Sarah was standing solo. This was my shot, and I wasn't going to miss it. I confidently walked up and stood next to her, always keeping one eye on the field as if I gave a shit about what was happening in the game.

"Hi, Sarah!"

"Hi," she replied.

...

...

...

"I love football!" I lied, hoping to spark conversation.

"Me too!"

...

...

...

"So, the fall formal is coming up and—"

Sarah smiled warmly and I felt like I was in, like she would say yes. My confidence shot through the roof immediately after I saw her flash her pearly whites. I took a beat, steadied my breath, and took both eyes off the field to look into her beautiful blues just as I heard an announcement over the loudspeaker...

"DANNY PELLEGRINO, YOUR PARENTS ARE LOOKING FOR YOU," the announcer said for everyone in the stadium to hear. I was mortified but determined to keep my cool in front of Sarah.

"That's you," Sarah said.

No shit.

"Do you need to go?" she asked.

"No, no, I'm sure it's fine. I'll go later," I assured. "So, about the dance...I was thinking—"

Before I could finish my sentence, I heard a more familiar voice echoing throughout the stadium. It was my mother.

"DAN, IT'S YOUR MOTHER. WE HAVE TO LEAVE EARLY, SO COME DOWN TO THE CONCESSION STAND! DANSTER? CAN YOU HEAR ME, DANSTER?" she said, her voice trailing off as the mic was taken from her hands.

"YOU HEAR THAT, DANSTER?" the announcer said with a laugh before getting back to the football game.

It was a nightmare. The entire student section looked over at me, laughing and pointing. While I wanted to run and hide, there was still a part of me trying to remain calm in front of the girl of my dreams. If I ran out of the stands in tears, I knew I would never recover. I'd be the kid no one wanted to befriend because he cried like a baby at the football game. Instead, I kept a smile on my face and laughed along with the other kids. It's always better to laugh at yourself before others do, and if you can't do it before them, do it with them. Psychologically, it might not be great for one's self-esteem, but it takes some of the power away from bullies.

"Does your mom always call you Danster?" Sarah asked.

"Yeah, it's an inside joke thing."

"What's the joke?" she followed up.

Truth is, it wasn't an inside joke, it was just something my mom called me since I was a young kid. One of those nicknames that stuck. It only occasionally snuck out of her mouth in public, unfortunately this time it happened over a microphone for the entire city to hear.

"Yeah, you know I better get going," I told Sarah, resigning the idea of finishing my mission and asking her to the dance. That ship had sailed. My only goal at this point was to walk off the bleachers, tell my parents I was never speaking to them again, and have them drive me home so I could listen to six more hours of a Brandy ballad, eat the stack of Airheads I hid under my mattress, and then cry again in the shower.

I walked toward the exit feeling low but keeping my head held high. I didn't want anyone to see how hurt I was that they were laughing and throwing metaphorical pig's blood on me like they did to Carrie at her prom or in *Jawbreaker*, when the crowd tossed corsages

at Rose McGowan. Seconds felt like hours as I inched my way toward
the bottom of the bleachers near the exit. On my way out, I heard the
familiar sounds of the cheer squad, who set up shop right in front of
the student section, spending the football game encouraging all students to root for the home team. Unfortunately, they took a break from
school spirit to drag me with an improvised cheer in perfect formation.

"Ready? Okay!" I heard the squad scream.

"D-A-N-S-T-E-R, your parents are looking for you, hey, your parents are looking for you!" they sang, finishing with one final "D-A-N-
S-T-E-R, DANSTER!"

It didn't quite rhyme, but it was impressive nonetheless that they
were able to make up something on the spot like that. Horrifying for
me though. Sometimes I close my eyes at night and hear the chant
playing over and over again in my head, wincing at the embarrassment
of it all. More laughs from the student section followed, along with
some finger-pointing from some parents and teachers that I knew as
I ran out of that stadium and made my way to the Brandy album as
quickly as time would allow.

Sarah and I never went to any dances together. She eventually
transferred schools and we lost touch, but I'll never forget that football
game and what a bunch of assholes the other students were, as well as
the cheerleading team and townspeople. Kids can be cruel, and while
I understand that others have had it way worse, I can't help but think
about how I felt that night. The confidence I had going into that game
was forever changed as I was leaving. Anytime I would try to flirt with
a girl after that, a familiar feeling of embarrassment would wash over
me. There were a handful of years where I dated girls and pretended

to be straight, but my flirt game never recovered until I came out of the closet.

The scars of our childhood never fully go away, and although we grow and learn, we never forget those wounds. Surely Sarah doesn't remember any of it, and Danster was, fortunately, not a nickname that stuck with my classmates. What did stick is the feeling of not being good enough. But looking back now, I realize that I was good enough. I *am* good enough, and very lucky that I had two parents who were looking for me. Now that I'm older, I still rely on Brandy to get through the tough times, only now I pair the *Full Moon* album with another brandy—cognac.

The Rain

"Nothing like a rainy day to reflect on
what a mess your life is, huh?"

JULIE COOPER, *THE O.C.*

It's always dicey when a loved one starts dating someone new. You could hate their latest significant other, they could hate you, or even worse...indifference. Indifference is the real sniper from the side, because if you don't like the person and don't hate the person, you have little energy to want to make any effort at all to spend time with them. Fortunately, both of my brothers ended up with women I adore like they are my own sisters, but it wasn't so easy to get where we're at now.

When Bryan started dating his now wife, I was still living with him. We were a brotherly duo who spent a lot of time together, and being that we were in our twenties, we had a lot of fun being friends as well as family. No matter who he started seeing at the time, it was going to be an adjustment for me and my relationship with him. He slowly started to bring his new girlfriend around more as they got to know each other, and all signs pointed to her being wonderful, so my focus was entirely on making sure that she liked me. This meant buttering her up with compliments, ordering extra food when I got takeout so she would feel included, and warming up to her dog, Teddy.

Teddy was the key to the whole relationship, as all pets are. If you want their owner to like you, just treat the dog like royalty. Easy enough, right? Dogs should be treated as such regardless but particularly when there's an added layer of impressing their parent. Teddy started to come to our shared condo more and more, just as my brother started falling more and more in love with Teddy's owner. They would both spend weekends at the house, but typically Teddy would go wherever they went if they left the house. He was a small dog, so he's easily able to hop on someone's lap and take a drive, but there was one Friday night they decided to leave him at the condo with me.

Bryan made their date night plans for dinner and a movie, and I offered to hang with the pooch while they were gone. It was an unusually chaotic weather night for northeast Ohio, as there was a hail/rain mix happening outside. I had just bought the first three seasons of *Entourage* on DVD, so I planned on having a quiet night in with Turtle and the gang, steering clear of the mess outdoors. Before you all judge me, just know that I'm opening my heart to you, and although *Entourage* is not looked back on very fondly by many today, it was, at that time, a critical HBO darling. We all watched it, so STOP. JUDGING. ME. PLEASE! Anyway, they left for their date, I fired up the DVD player, watched a few eps with some ramen, and enjoyed my low-key evening. Unfortunately, while I was enjoying Vince and

Drama's crazy Hollywood antics, I spilled some soup on my shirt like the dummy I am.

Our washer/dryer was located right by the door that led to the garage, which is where Teddy spent most of his time, waiting for his mama to return from her date. I decided to do a full load of laundry, so I carried my basket of clothes to the area and put them in the machine. At that point, Teddy hadn't quite warmed up to me yet, constantly barking at my mere presence, and I don't fault him for it. Without getting into too much detail about his rescue story, he wasn't a big fan of male energy. Who among us is, really? He was also fiercely protective of his owner, so anytime anyone was near her and he could see them, he would bark and bark and bark. Teddy woofed at me as I put my clothes in the washer, but I did my best to ignore it. My plan was to throw everything into the machine, including my ramen-soaked shirt, and then take a nice, long shower before settling in for some more of Ari and E's on-screen tension. I took everything off other than my boxer-briefs, ran the wash, and headed to my loft, where I was out of Teddy's way, hoping he would quit barking.

As I made my way to the shower, I heard three things: Teddy's barking, the *Entourage* theme song playing on repeat over the DVD menu—which consisted of a lot of *oh yeahs*—and the sound of the rain/hail mix inside the garage. I knew that meant my brother forgot to close the garage door when he left, or perhaps the crazy weather got in the way of the sensor and stopped it from shutting. Either way, I wanted to make sure it was closed before I got in the shower, so I went back toward the garage door in my underwear to press the button and ensure things were closed.

When I opened the door that led to the garage, Teddy decided to run out, still inside the garage, but no longer inside the house. I freaked out.

"Teddy, come here, boy! Come back inside!" I said, silently praying he would listen.

Instead, he just stood still. I continued to call him, inching my way out the door, closer and closer to him in just my underwear. He wasn't taking my bait and decided to run out into the yard. It was dark and hailing outside, but I couldn't let him run away, not on my watch. I grabbed the nearest boots in the garage, an old pair my brother used for construction, and walked toward Teddy. I knew I would get wet, but I figured it was just the front yard and my health wasn't as concerning as getting this dog inside. Teddy inched farther away from me.

The entire relationship with my future sister-in-law flashed before my eyes. She would never forgive me if I was responsible for something happening to her baby, and how could she? The problem is, every time I got closer to Teddy, he scurried, and he was a quick little doggie. I'm no speed racer, and the oversize work boots I had on weren't helping, but I did my best. Pretty soon I was in the next-door neighbor's yard, then I was down the street, then the next street over, and finally in the woods somewhere, yards away from our home. Teddy was so fast that I couldn't catch up, and although I was able to keep my eye on him for a long stretch, I just couldn't seem to get him to stop or come to me. He was probably terrified that a grown man in underwear and clown shoes was chasing after him in the rain, but I had no choice!

When we got into the woods, I didn't have the assistance of the streetlamps to help me see him. It was too dark and too late; Teddy was officially lost. Since I ran out of the house without any clothes, it also meant I didn't have my phone. This was during my cell phone belt clip era, so when I didn't have a waistline, I didn't have my Nokia. Flashbacks of my sixth-grade slumber party debacle came rushing in my head. I've been through some shit in my life, but this moment was truly one of the worst because I had no idea what to do. My only glimmer of hope was that I've watched *Homeward Bound* and *Homeward Bound II: Lost in San Francisco* so many times that I knew if Sassy the cat could survive a waterfall and the West Coast, Teddy could maybe make it through the Ohio rain. I wasn't sure if I should stay in the forest, trembling and almost naked and hope to find Teddy, or if I should go back home to call for backup, put on some clothes, and find him that way. Neither one seemed all that great, but I opted to head back to the condo.

On the way, I walked through the streets yelling his name in case he started to head that way too. He didn't show up, but the headlights on a familiar car did. I squinted behind me at the vehicle driving my way; it was my brother. They decided to skip the movie and come home after dinner. He slowed as he drove close and opened the window.

"What the fuck?" he asked. Actually, I'm not sure that those were his exact words, but it was something like that. There was a "what the fuck" energy to the moment, for sure. I honestly looked crazy, almost naked and soaking wet, but not like in a sexy way. This wasn't Britney's "Stronger" video—I was a hot mess, and now I had to deliver the bad news to the happy couple.

"I opened the garage door and Teddy ran out. I tried to run after him, but he—" The words shook out of me, my body in fight-or-flight mode from the cold night. Seeing their faces left me even colder. There's no easy way to tell someone you lost their dog. I got in the car and they drove me home, telling me to go inside and call my parents to come help look for Teddy, and also to put on some clothes, while they drove the car back to the wooded area in the neighborhood to look for him.

Walking back into the empty house made me wish Teddy were there barking at me. What I would've given to hear the sound of that little doggie instead of the still-playing *oh yeahs* of disc one of season 3B of *Entourage*.

My parents lived close by, so they immediately came to help, and so did my other brother and his wife. We all scoured the neighborhood with flashlights, looking for the scared pooch in the pouring rain. As much as I was worried about what this would mean for my relationship with my brother's new girlfriend, I was even more terrified for Teddy being out there all alone at night. I thought about the asshole previous owner who conditioned this beautiful little dog to be so scared of other people. Animal abuse is a larger issue than we have time for here, but it's truly abhorrent that people could treat creatures that way.

As our search party perused the streets, I kept apologizing. With fresh clothes on, I was doing my best to focus on our rescue, and eventually, thank God (Mariah Carey), that my dad found Teddy underneath a parked car, shivering close to the back left tire. He was scared, and although he would usually run from men, Teddy this time sat still, allowing my dad to wrap him up and bring him home. I have never felt such relief. He was safe.

My brother eventually asked Teddy's mom to move into the condo when I moved off to Chicago. They got married, had three kids, and

lived happily ever after. Teddy is still around and has calmed down
a bit, but not so much with me. When I see him, my energy is completely off, and I think he can sense that. I try my best, bringing him
treats for the holidays and petting him as much as he'll let me, but our
relationship has been tainted. The memories of that night come flooding back when I see his sweet face, and I'm sure it's the same for him.
He barks and I shudder, feeling like I'm back in my underwear running
through the sleet-filled street, the sound of the *Entourage* theme song
playing in my head.

"Oh yeah," I think to myself in the singsong way of the DVD menu.

A few days after Teddy ran away, my brother and I received a
flier in the mail that had gone out to every mailbox in the neighborhood. It was a grainy image of me that looked like it was taken with
a Razr phone, the word WARNING in big, bold letters above the
photo. "A man was seen running through the neighborhood in his
underwear, yelling at the top of his lungs. Please report if seen again,"
the flier said.

Turns out whoever saw me didn't see Teddy that night either. They simply saw a lunatic on the brink of a breakdown. They saw me for exactly who I was.

Magic Mike

We all cope with tragedy differently, and I don't think there's a right or wrong way to do it. My hope is we can all hold each other's hands throughout the sadness that life gives us and offer each other grace as we go through the process. Maybe that makes me seem like that character in *Mean Girls* who just wants to make a cake of rainbows for everyone, but it's how I feel. Our time is hard enough without the unexpected events that can break our spirits. It's important we all have shoulders to lean on, strength to keep moving forward, and friends to help us find the laughter when it feels impossible to smile.

Leaving my family and friends in the Midwest when I entered adulthood was always a difficult decision for me. My parents live one street over from both my brothers and their families, and they all work together too, so me wanting to fly across the country to live my life never made much sense to them. Many of my childhood friends have also set up shop in Ohio, so it becomes a challenge to keep in touch with them while I live in California. Part of me always figured I would end up back there after a few years of adventures in my twenties and thirties, and while I still haven't decided to make the move back, I do find time to spend with my loved ones, usually meeting in Las Vegas for debauched days in a casino. It's an easy forty-five-minute plane ride from Los Angeles, and flights from Ohio to Vegas are cheap, so it's convenient to meet people there, catch up for a few days, and then go back to the real world.

One of my lifelong best friends, Katie, now lives in Columbus, Ohio, but in 2017, we decided to have a frienaissance in Sin City. She's a nurse, and my schedule is all over the place, so we weren't able to do a proper weekend; instead we planned to fly in on Sunday and have three nights together in a cheap hotel room. We had aspirations of sitting at a slot machine, drinking countless vodka sodas, and eating at buffets. What we got was quite different.

I was first to arrive, Sunday morning, while Katie's flight was due to get in early afternoon, so I had time to check into our hotel at Planet Hollywood on the strip, get some lunch, and unwind.

"I don't want to spend too much time gambling. Let's see a show tonight to keep us off the tables! Can you check to see what tickets are available?" Katie asked me over the phone from the airport.

"Sure," I said before heading to the hotel concierge.

On my way downstairs, I browsed one of those pamphlets I carried with me from the inside of a cab that listed every magician, comedian, pop star, and dance show on the strip. It was an overwhelming selection. The concierge helped me out, telling me there were no divas (Mariah, Céline, Britney) playing that Sunday night, but there were some hot tickets, namely Magic Mike Live, a country music festival, and a Cirque du Soleil–esque dance show. I was about to buy the country festival tickets for the both of us when Katie texted me that her flight was delayed. She wouldn't arrive at the hotel until around seven, so it would be tough to make it to anything other than the late show of Magic Mike Live.

Detour

I LOVE *Magic Mike* with all my heart and soul. Channing Tatum's performance as a male stripper was revolutionary, one of the greatest in the history of cinema. No man has ever moved on screen the way that he did, and I'm not sure any man will ever again. How the Academy didn't shower his fine ass with awards, I'll never know. Of course, I liked Chan when he burst onto screen in the underrated Amanda Bynes vehicle, *She's the Man* and the wonderful *Step Up*, but nothing could have prepared me for the magnetism that he would display as an exotic dancer who also made furniture and even did drag in that one random sequence in the first film. While I don't remember any plot points of that first movie, I do remember his "Pony" dance, a sequence that will live rent free in my mind for all of eternity. I'll be on my death bed thinking of the subtle way he thrust his junk into the face of a blessed extra. His red thong should be hung in the Louvre, and dancing should be outlawed, *Footloose* style, until every man can move like him. *Magic Mike XXL*, the second film, continued the story of Channing as Mike, and it's an almost flawless movie, my only complaint is that there isn't enough nudity for a stripper tale. My understanding is that women prefer the tease and don't want to see the full male body on display. I remember watching a segment on *The View* discussing the *Fifty Shades of Grey* movies and how Jamie Dornan wasn't showing his full Peter Rabbit, while his female costar Dakota Johnson showed her Meredith Grey, and the entire panel actually said on air that they didn't want to see his disco stick. The double standard was obvious to me, but the ladies argued that women weren't interested in seeing full penis. Many of my girlfriends feel differently, so I'm not sure I believe that, but I can tell you with 100 percent confidence that gay men DO want to see the full male body on display. At the very least, we want to see Matt Bomer in a thong for multiple scenes/frames, and *Magic Mike XXL* didn't give us enough of that in my opinion. Regardless, I hold both films to high esteem and will defend them to my death.

Channing opted to take the *Magic Mike* film franchise to the stage, and not since *The Lion King* on Broadway has there been such a seamless film-to-stage adaptation. The idea that people could descend upon Vegas from all parts of the world and see this IP with the lax Vegas liquor laws is…chef's kiss. I was so excited for a night of abs with one of my very best friends.

When Katie finally got to the hotel, there was just enough time for her to shower and shove some food in her mouth before we headed to the Hard Rock Hotel for the hot, naked men show. The cocktails started flowing the moment her suitcase was wheeled into our room, so we were nicely lubricated by the time we got to the ticket will call.

The show started beautifully, with sexy lighting and a server who took our drink orders before we even sat in our seats. We opted to get the fishbowl-size vodka sodas, reasoning that we had already started drinking hard liquor, so even though the glasses were big enough to house a living creature, at least we weren't mixing different types of alcohol like wine or beer. I'm here to tell you that no one actually needs a drink that big. You might think you do, but you don't. Never. There's no occasion where that makes sense. Just have one human-size drink and then order another if you're still thirsty or not buzzed enough. A fishbowl should be for fish, not vodka, but I'm 100 percent certain that I will again make the same mistake in the future.

Drinks were flowing so freely that I couldn't tell you if there was a story line on stage or if the men were simply taking off their blouses for the audience to ogle. I blacked out the details, but I do remember the men were gorgeous, and the hostess gave everyone in the audience paper money that was like Monopoly dollars, only instead of buying hotels for Boardwalk Empire, you used it to make it rain on a man whose baby-maker you wanted to see up close and personal. I also remember the crowd, filled with women and gay men hooting and hollering in a way that can only be described as unspeakably horny. If straight men had any sense (they don't), they would hang outside the venue, waiting for the show to end, because everyone's motor is running during Magic Mike Live.

There's no real easy way to transition here, but about three quarters of the way through the show, just when Katie and I were starting to see double and order triples, I got a text from a friend who lived in the area. Her husband is a police officer in Las Vegas, and she said that he just got word that there was an active shooter on the strip. News like that is sobering, to say the least. The woman next to me was shouting, "Show me your dick," at a dancer, while I was trying to read a terrifying, albeit blurry to my drunk eyes, text. I showed Katie and neither one of us knew exactly how to react.

"Should we leave?" I asked Katie.

"I'm sure it's nothing, let's just get another drink," she replied, waving down our server for another fishbowl.

I texted my friend for more details, put my phone in my pocket, and continued waving my paper money at the nearest topless man. News like that is often hard for me to digest, and I naively assumed it was all an overexaggeration or misreported. Surely it was nothing because nothing bad like that ever happens in Vegas, a place of pure adult joy...right? We put reason aside and finished the show.

As soon as we exited the dark lights of the theater, we knew something was really wrong. We all, unfortunately, now know how the evening ultimately played out, but at the time, things weren't so clear. Casinos are always a little hectic, but word was traveling fast that there was an active shooter nearby, and everyone in the casino was visibly terrified. While the Hard Rock Hotel is off the strip and far away from Mandalay Bay, where the shooting took place, there wasn't a lot of concrete info as to what was actually happening. People were running around, scared, some yelling, others telling people that there were attacks at other casinos. Our first instinct was to get a hotel room at Hard Rock, as we didn't want to go closer to where this was all happening, in case that would put us in more danger. It seemed like the best course of action was to stay put in one spot, away from the crowds. The line for reservations filled up quick, but we were able to book one of the remaining open rooms.

Next we went to the gift shop to get some essentials for the night.

We wouldn't know how long we would be in our room, so we grabbed the basics...toothbrushes, contact lens solution, and because we were hammered, snacks upon snacks upon snacks. All the while, pure chaos erupted around us. As I waited in line, I called my parents, who were asleep. I told them to turn on the news and promised them Katie and I would go to our room and keep them posted when we knew more. Texts started coming in from friends and family who knew we were both in town. I texted back everyone I could, letting them know I was fine and at a hotel.

Katie, drunk as she was, decided to post on social media to let her network of people know she was okay before her phone battery died. It would've made sense for her to update her Facebook status or her Twitter feed with something like, "I'm okay! Will check in when I know more," but she had deleted Facebook and Twitter a few days earlier, so IG was the only platform at her disposal. Obviously, you have to post a picture on IG, so she couldn't just update the caption with her where-abouts. While I would've opted to post a Notes app update or a blank screen with information in the caption, Katie uploaded the most recent photo in her camera roll, which happened to be an accidental screen-shot of her iPhone screen. She posted it with the caption, "My only form of social media at this point. Phone is about to die. I'm safe. At the Hard Rock Hotel in Vegas. I'll contact loved ones when I can." Almost immediately her phone battery ran out, and since we didn't have chargers at our new hotel, that was the last communication we had with people. That accidental screenshot was all her people saw throughout the entire night. In the screengrab (shown on the next page), you can see an email she got from Zazzle, and another from Groupon.

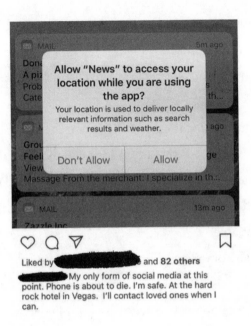

Comments immediately flooded in underneath the photo, people saying things like, "wtf is this photo?" or "is that an email from Zazzle?" as they tried to extract extra meaning behind Katie's picture during such a tumultuous time.

In the gift shop, I grabbed every Kit Kat they had, paid, and went straight to our room. The tragic events were not happening where we were exactly, but again, we didn't know anything other than what people were saying on the casino floor. In our new hotel room, we put on the news and watched in horror as the events unfolded so closely to us and new information trickled out. I'll never understand how anyone could be so heartless, so evil.

Everything that transpired sobered us up, so we didn't wake up still tipsy like we normally would have. We exited the Hard Rock Hotel that next morning, and the Vegas strip felt like a ghost town.

Normally the street is bustling at every hour with people, laughing and smiling or angry about money lost at the craps table. Instead, a sense of sadness filled the city. A former adult Disneyland was now a place of lingering devastation.

Even as sadness filled the air for lives lost, there was a sense of perseverance that permeated the city. Video billboards that once advertised Boys II Men and Carrot Top were now showing "Vegas Strong," reminding residents and visitors that it will get through the darkness. It was nonnegotiable.

We were like zombies walking through the motions that next day, thinking of how easily it could've been us at that concert and thinking about how those people who died were people just looking for some time away with their own best friends.

Katie and I contemplated flying to our respective homes early, but that didn't quite feel right. It might be years before we were able to spend quality time together again, and there was a comforting collective mourning that was happening in town that I'm not sure I can put into words. I wonder if the people who think anyone should be able to own an assault rifle would still feel that way if they were able to be in Las Vegas that morning. Maybe they would think differently if they could feel the unspeakable loss that hung in the air.

With our trip still in progress, and every live show canceled on Monday night, we decided to order some drinks to the room and try to have a dance party. To be honest, we didn't know what to do. Maybe it was inappropriate of us to dance? We had spent the day tense and sad. I'm not a religious person, but I prayed for all the lives lost and the families who were finding out that they had lost loved ones. In our hotel room, we put on the TV and every channel was dedicated to the events of the night before. I felt helpless and trapped in sorrow. *Grey's Anatomy* has taught me that dancing it out is self-care, so we put on Mariah Carey and did our best to lift our spirits as much as we could. Eventually, we made our way to the casino floor, where many others were trying to force on a smile just as we were. Slots and blackjack only did so much, and we needed to do something to get our minds off the events. Enter a psychic.

Psychics have long fascinated me, usually from a distance. It seemed like a fun, spontaneous thing to take our minds off the sadness. Katie felt similarly, and although we thought it would be easy to find one in Vegas, it turns out there aren't a ton on the strip. We sat at a casino bar, scrolling the internet on our phones for the closest clairvoyant.

"I'm gonna run to the restroom," I said to Katie.

By the time I got back a few moments later, Katie had already booked us an appointment and ordered a car that would take us off the strip. Way off. The drive to our reading was almost an hour. We ended up in a small town outside of Vegas, empty and desolate, pulling up to a small apartment complex with no streetlights and very little sign of life. We should've turned right around, but instead we got out of the car and Katie texted the woman she had been communicating with who was set to give us a reading.

The woman, who told us her name was Xelcius, led us into her home, where Fox News was playing on the TV in her living room for her daughter, who looked roughly ten.

"You first," Xelcius said to Katie, bringing her into her bedroom as I sat on the couch in her living room. How we just went along with all of this is beyond me. There were so many red flags, reasons we should've bounced, but we did whatever Xelcius told us.

Rather than make small talk with the child who was watching Tucker Carlson, I decided to get on my phone, text friends, and take some photos of our whereabouts. I thought it was important to document the occasion, not just for safety, but so future me could remember what happened this night, as I would surely try to block it out of memory.

Katie finished up and Xelcius asked me to step in her room.

"I'm gay!" I shouted as I entered, a fight-or-flight response, in effort to erase any potential sexual tension that could arise as she asked me to sit on her bed for the reading. I was wearing a Britney Spears shirt and a light layer of concealer, so there's little reason to think she wouldn't have known I was homosexual, but I told her anyway. As I sat on her bed, my faith in her psychic abilities was nonexistent. I wanted to get in and get out, satisfied that Katie and I would have this batshit story without needing any sort of tarot card thing.

"You have a show," she said, eyes closed while holding my hand.

"That show is going to grow. You'll have celebrity guests and go on the road. It will open many doors for you," she continued.

I thought it was all bullshit. I left the room, rolling my eyes for only Katie to see, and politely smiled at Xelcius as we left her apartment.

"Did you tell her I started a podcast?" I asked Katie.

"No, why would I talk to a psychic about a podcast?" she countered.

Our effort to take our minds off the grief fell flat, and the whole psychic experience made me feel gross. Gross that we had spent so much money, gross that we drove so far for so little, and gross that we were on this trip in the first place when tragedy struck so many people. There was also an air of guilt that we were able to continue when so many others were no longer afforded the opportunity.

We both looked out our windows on our ride back to the strip, thinking about everything that transpired over our two nights. A tear flowed out of my eye, a culmination of every emotion, and then, unexpectedly, I heard Katie laugh. Not just any laugh, it was the laugh I first fell in love with when we met as young teenagers, familiar, warm, and infectious. It was the chuckle that I remember hearing at fourteen when we went on a student council trip and the one I remember hearing at eighteen when we got tipsy after our high school graduation. Before the tear could even dry on my cheek, I joined her, laughing for the first time since we arrived. I wasn't sure what I was initially even laughing at, but it happened, and it was the church giggles, the kind of laugh that you know that you shouldn't be participating in but trying to stop it only makes you laugh even more. The sad tears and happy tears combined into a release. The rest of the car ride was filled with those laughs, the kind only two close friends find together that you would never be able to explain to anyone else. We laughed at Katie's absurd and inappropriate Instagram post and at our ridiculous psychic visit. We laughed and laughed and laughed. When we planned our trip, we expected to have a traditional visit...slots, booze, and shows. We had all those things, but it was anything but traditional. Every time I had a milestone with my podcast, I thought about the tarot cards, and the prediction, and in turn, Katie. I'm still not sure I believe in Xelcius, but I believe in the power of a frienaissance, reuniting with an old friend for a fun time.

So many lives were horrifically lost in that shooting, sixty in total. Countless friendships broken, robbed of the kind of laughs we were so fortunate to have on our ride back to the hotel. My heart will forever hurt thinking of the people who were tragically killed and the loved ones they left behind, but if you're reading this and thinking of your Katie, a person you don't get to see as much as you want, I'm here to remind you to book that trip. Meet them somewhere and make some memories while you still can, because you never know when you won't be able to anymore. Life is hard and short, and in the end, those friendships are all we have.

The Tooth Cleaning

"Oops."

KIM RICHARDS, *THE REAL HOUSEWIVES OF BEVERLY HILLS*

Who among us hasn't stress eaten a full bag of caramels during a presidential debate? I certainly have, and while I was eating during the last election, I noticed something loose in my tooth. Rather than stop chewing on the hell candy, I decided to eat more and hope the next caramels I shoved in my mouth would somehow adhere the loose item in my mouth to whatever it was loose from. The mechanics of my decision-making weren't quite worked out, but whatevs, I'm a dummy sometimes.

"I have to go to the dentist. My tooth fell out!" I shouted at my boyfriend at 11:00 p.m.

"It's fine, it's just your filling."

"But it looks just like a whole tooth!"

"It's supposed to look like your teeth," he said.

While he was trying to calm me down, I used my tongue to inspect the area. I took GREAT care of my chompers, save for bingeing candy when I'm emotional, and I've never had braces or a retainer. The one filling I did have was done at such a young age, I had forgotten it was even a thing.

My fear led me to the internet, which can be an incredibly dangerous place. I get myself into enough trouble when I'm on eBay buying *Space Jam* merch or looking for rare *Tiny Toons* Happy Meal toys from my youth, but I'm a whole other level of dangerous when I'm googling symptoms or ailments. A mere moment went by before I found myself on a message board for mouth care. Someone on the page suggested that when a filling falls out, you should wrap it up and bring it to the dentist, so I immediately put it in a tissue and took an old Xanax that I found in the medicine cabinet so I could fall asleep.

The next morning, I called my dentist and told them it was an absolute emergency (it wasn't). Keep in mind it was fall of 2020, when COVID-19 and the election were in full swing. EMOTIONS WERE HIGH, and I hadn't communicated much with people in person most of the year. Going to the dentist was one of the few times I left the house aside from going to the grocery store, so I put on my finest wares and made it a special event. There was a new button-down I had bought right before quarantine, so I threw that on, tossed my dead filling in my shirt pocket, gelled my hair, and pressed my pants. I looked like a million bucks.

My dentist took a quick look at my teeth and suggested refilling, without any need for my old one, so that old toothlike thing that I had wrapped in a tissue the way my grandma used to wrap a half-eaten cough drop was sitting tight in my shirt. The doc finished up the work on my mouth and I headed back home.

A few days later, I decided to run some errands. There was a tote bag of clothes that I wanted to take to the dry cleaners and some mail I had to drop at the box, so I gathered my things and left the house.

Going anywhere during the first year of the pandemic was a challenge, navigating new rules and guidelines at places you've been a hundred times. At the dry cleaners, they put those little feet stickers on the ground indicating where to stand in line so you would always be at least six feet away from the other customers. I hopped onto one of the stickers, behind an older woman with kind eyes and what looked like seventeen pillowcases she was having dry-cleaned and in front of an older gentleman I could tell was gay because we were in West Hollywood, and he also had a tote bag with two cartoon men kissing on it and literally said *I'M A BIG GAY* in bold letters. I wish I knew where he got that bag...

The woman in front of me finished up, and I started walking to the register, simultaneously pulling out my clothes to present to the cashier. As I yanked the shirts out of my bag, the old filling I had forgotten was wrapped in a tissue in one of the pockets got loose and floated to the floor of the dry cleaners. As I bent down to grab it, I saw the toothlike filling roll out of the tissue and tumble to the feet of the old man with the horny tote.

Instinctively, he picked up the filling and reached his hand out toward me as his eyes began to inspect what was now in his hands in the midst of a global pandemic.

"What's this?" he said as his arm extended into the six-foot radius measured out for me by the dry cleaners.

"That's my old tooth filling," I responded.

Color immediately escaped this man's face like Reese Witherspoon in the movie *Pleasantville*, as if he just saw a ghost. His hand nervously tossed my old mouthpiece into the air as he let out a scream that can only be described as a turkey running for freedom on Thanksgiving morning.

As the filling drifted in the wind, the woman that had once been in front of me in line was now dodging the loose tooth figurine like she was Keanu Reeves in *The Matrix* or Ghostface dodging a saucer that Anna Faris's character threw at him in the *Scary Movie* scene that parodies *The Matrix*.

Under normal circumstances, I would've pushed everyone aside so I could grab the item, then put it in my pocket, run out of the establishment, and cry in the shower while listening to a Mary J. Blige ballad. But this was a pandemic. I had to keep a social distance.

The filling then hit the ground for a second time, and I got on my hands and knees, but it continued to roll away from me. I can only assume they had waxed the floors right before my visit, because that thing was moving faster than lightning. Eventually, I caught up to it and let out a sigh of relief.

"Oops. Forgot that was in my shirt pocket," I said to the other patrons, who looked at me like I was crazed.

Since I'd already embarrassed myself, I figured I might as well get my clothes cleaned. I dragged my belongings to the register and unloaded my clothes on the counter with the dead filling tightly in my grasp so it wouldn't do any more bouncing.

"Just the six shirts and two pairs of pants, ready by Friday would be great," I informed the cashier.

"You don't have any other...teeth in the pockets, do you?" she asked.

"No, just the one," I said, "and it was just a filling."

She handed me a receipt and I started to walk toward the door with my head down, horrified.

I glanced up at the old man. He lifted his mask and smiled. It wasn't a happy smile, he grinned just enough so I could see mouth.

"Dentures," he said. "You're lucky you have teeth to fill."

Always count your blessings.

How Can We Be Lovers

Music is like a time machine that can transport us to specific moments in life. I did dinner theater in Chicago, and every time I hear "YMCA," I'm suddenly in the Windy City. The beautiful eight-bit sounds of *Super Mario Bros.* can take me to Christmas morning 1990, and when I hear the *Mulan* soundtrack, the sadness of my middle school years washes over me and I'm standing with my choir teacher who took away my "I'll Make a Man Out of You" solo moments before the choral concert. My college years are loaded with special songs, one in particular that will always hold a special place in my heart and emotionally carry me right back to my freshman year.

When I arrived in Athens, Ohio, for my first year of college, I was excited to start fresh. Even though Athens is a small town, it was a big city to me. I had spent my entire life in a suburb of Cleveland, so going to the other side of the state felt like a huge deal. Plus, *Love & Basketball* was one of my favorite movies, so despite not playing a sport or having a significant other, I was delighted to enter the dramatic "third quarter" portion of my life, like Quincy and Monica did when they got to college. All I was missing was a meal card, a girlfriend (I was *still* in the closet), and a tiny basketball hoop in my dormitory to play strip basketball. I eventually got the meal card.

One of the requirements my freshman year was to take a language course. I chose American Sign Language (ASL) hoping to better connect with a new friend who was deaf. The class, pre-final, went by swimmingly. The professor was a woman in her forties who was tough and intelligent, but she didn't seem to have a funny bone in her body. I tend to find the humor in everything, and this woman never cracked a smile. Not a chuckle to be found within spitting distance of this woman. She was like an episode of *Homeland*. People who don't have a sense of humor leave me uneasy, but my grades were consistently good throughout the year, and I proved to myself I had the ability to learn another language. It may sound stupid, but it felt like a new world opened to me. Plus, one of my new besties, Jenny, was in the class with me.

Because I was thriving, I got maybe a little too comfortable in the class. Some confidence is good, but too much can lead you down a bad path. Toward the end of the year, the professor dropped the bomb on us.

"For the final exam, you must sign a children's book in front of the class," she said.

I turned to Jenny and we began spitballing book ideas. She mentioned Dr. Seuss, while I wondered if *Where the Wild Things Are* would be too long for a presentation. As we were talking, another student raised their hand.

"Do we have to do a book?" he asked.

"You can do a song, just bring in the music and you can sign along with it."

Music seemed like more work, so I shrugged it off and thought about more book ideas. We had a week before the presentation, so I figured I would go to the library and find something easy that would also impress. Class ended that day, and Jenny and I headed straight back to the dorm rooms.

Detour

Dorm living is the best. My favorite part was the communal aspect of watching television. I'll never forget the entire floor watching the season two finale of *Grey's Anatomy*. Izzie and Denny had a love story for the ages. I could cry right now thinking of Katherine Heigl in a merlot-colored dress, cozying up to the dead body of Jeffrey Dean Morgan while Snow Patrol played in the background. BRB going to get some tissues...

...back.

Our dorm floor also loved *American Idol*. We kept a journal during the season, and we would write down all the batshit things Paula Abdul said after performances. I personally don't think the show ever recovered from Paula's leave. That original panel was magic. Magic! I eventually returned to watch the Mariah Carey season, but nothing compared to Ms. Abdul saying nonsensical things at hopeful young singers. Remember that time she critiqued a performance that had yet to happen on the live show?

THAT MOMENT IS WHY I LOVE TELEVISION.

When the other judges and Seacrest corrected her, she seemed stunned. If you don't know what I'm talking about, go YouTube it. I'm not saying she was a mess, but I am implying it.

Anyway, back to my ASL class. This course was my last class of the day, so often, Jenny and I would leave and meet up with friends for boozing. This particular night, we decided to do one of those "power hours" in the dorm. If you're not familiar, it's a drinking game where you listen to music and the song changes every sixty seconds. Each time it does, you drink. Someone had the bright idea to do it with liquor as a challenge, so every sixty seconds, we would take a sip of the cheapest vodka we could find. I'm constantly concerned with "gut health" now that I'm in my thirties, but back then I would chug from a nine-dollar liter of gas station liquor that tasted like old feet. By minute fifty, we were wasted and singing at the top of our lungs. This particular Power Hour was a '90s theme, so every minute would be a different song from the era. One of the last was Michael Bolton's "How Can We Be Lovers," which was released in 1990, so it just barely made the cut. It's one of those songs that not every-one necessarily loves but everyone accidentally knows every lyric to, like "All Star" by Smash Mouth. Jenny and I were singing along and having the best time when she joked that it would be funny if one of us performed it for the ASL final. We quickly laughed it off and fin-ished the power hour.

After the sixty-minute mark, we all headed off to the bar. There was a place on campus that was eighteen and over and known for being lax with fake IDs, so we spent most of freshman year there. They also had a pool table and jukebox that made it a welcoming establish-ment for the older townies, so it was great for people-watching too. When we got there, Jenny and I were just drunk enough to think we would have a successful pool game and also so drunk that we would actually have a terrible pool game. We had spent an hour consuming the foot vodka, so we racked the balls and decided to make things interesting.

"What should we bet?" I slurred.

"A bet, huh? How about whoever wins gets to pick what the other person does for their ASL final," she replied.

"Deal!"

It's important to note that we could barely stand at this point, let alone play pool. I think it took us about an hour just to finish the game, and I looked like one of those inflatable tube men stationed in front of car dealerships as I waited my turn.

Jenny won.

As she was thinking about what song to make me sign for my ASL final, another friend was playing a song on the jukebox. It was Khia's "My Neck, My Back."

"Do this song!" Jenny shouted.

Don't get me wrong, that song is a forever bop, but it's hardly appropriate to sign about a pussy and a crack in a classroom setting.

"I can't do this. I'm not signing a song about my pussy and my crack," I reasoned.

"But that's the bet. You lost, so you have to sign about your pussy and your crack," she replied.

"I'm sorry, but it's too far. The professor will fail me the moment I sign about licking my—"

"They play it on the radio!" Jenny interrupted.

"Not with the 'pussy and crack' in it, it's censored!" I argued.

"Forget it."

"No, I lost the bet. Fair is fair. I'll do any song that doesn't have 'pussy and crack' in it. Anything else."

"Fine, then do the Michael Bolton song," Jenny said.

"'How Can We Be Lovers'?"

"Yeah. There are no swear words."

"Deal. I'll do that one," I said.

Eventually we stumbled back to the dorms, our feet chaotically stomping around campus like two baby giraffes fresh out of the womb.

The next morning, I woke up fresh as a daisy because...youth. I spent the afternoon debating in my head if the Michael Bolton song would be appropriate to sign. The word *lovers* felt sort of weird, but, again, at least it wasn't Khia. I gave in and spent the week learning to sign it.

Jenny and I eventually headed off to our ASL final. She had prepared *One Fish, Two Fish, Red Fish, Blue Fish* by Dr. Seuss, and I had memorized the power ballad about making love after making amends with a scorned partner. On the way, we theorized what other students would do, figuring at least a few others would do music.

We arrived at the classroom and there were a bunch of older people who looked like my parents in the room. Seated in front of the adults, there were very young children, around age six to eight. I assumed either they, or I, had walked into the wrong classroom.

The professor walked in and closed the door behind her. Apparently, I was in the right place and so were all the adults and young children filling up the space.

"Welcome to the ASL final, books away. Today you will be signing your prepared children's story. I've brought in some guests to help judge your work, so please say hello to the Deaf Boys and Girls Club of Southeast Ohio," the professor said.

Shit.

I thought I would be performing a Michael Bolton song for a classroom of college students, not six-year-olds. I was already on the fence about signing my chosen-for-me song, so I raised my hand to ask if I could do it privately. The professor pointed at me and when I began to ask my question, she signed something back that I didn't understand in my anxiety haze.

"She said we're only to use sign for the remainder of class," Jenny whispered.

"I can't sign Michael Bolton to a group of deaf children," I told her.

I looked to my left and saw the smiling faces of kids ready to be entertained.

The professor instructed the first student to stand and start. That young woman got up in front of the group and signed *The Cat in the Hat*. Another student followed with *Goodnight Moon*. The man who asked about doing a song was next. My heart rate slowed as I anticipated his performance. Since he was the one who asked to do a song, surely he was doing some pop music, right? He popped his CD into the CD player at the front of the room and signed along to "Old MacDonald." Old MacDonald. What the fuck? I thought he would do a Ludacris song or maybe the Pussycat Dolls...SOMETHING popular and on the radio at the time. Not Old Mac-motherfucking-Donald. Jenny went next and, of course, slayed her Dr. Seuss performance with ease.

As Jenny was wrapping up, I wanted to leave my body. Remember that movie *Under the Tuscan Sun* with Diane Lane, where she escapes her existence and starts a new life in Tuscany? I was ready to run out of that classroom and buy a villa. If only I had more than seven dollars in my bank account. It was so rude of Diane Lane to present that perfect film to us, knowing I couldn't afford to live out my own version of the story. Every other student signed a kid's book. Did no one else hear her say that we could do a song? Did she say only a "nursery rhyme" or book? I was sweating profusely, and my heart was beating out of my chest. The only thing that calmed me down was knowing I wouldn't be signing about my pussy and my crack.

Rather than risk failing the class, I went up to the stage...I mean, I went up to the front of the classroom. I popped my CD in and waved to the children as the opening chords of Michael Bolton's "How Can We Be Lovers" began to play. When I looked up, I saw one of the parents smiling ear to ear before the lyrics even started. She was a good time gal, I could tell. And it comforted me imagining that she likely met one of her ex-husbands back in 1991 when she was drunk on whiskeys with a single splash of Diet Coke at a local dive bar. I could see on her face that the song brought back great memories for her. I like to think her birth name was Eleanor, but she changed it to Vyper or Sprindelle in the '80s. I wish I knew where Vyper is now, but I digress.

The other adults looked bewildered when the power ballad kicked into high gear. I began to sign alongside the big-haired crooner, trepidatious at first. One of the parents covered the eyes of her child, while another shook their head in disgust as I signed about lovers. By the second chorus, I was in the zone. I imagine it was how Queen Britney

Spears felt when she performed songs off her album *In the Zone*. For the most part, the children just looked grossed out and certainly didn't seem to enjoy it in the slightest. I once tried to watch the movie *Donnie Darko* at my friend's house, and his grandma decided to watch with us. It's a very dark, often confusing, artistic film. She spent the first half hour looking at the screen the way someone looks at their spouse when that spouse farts in bed. That was basically how those kids looked at me. Disgusted. Like they were my friend's grandmother, and I was the first half hour of *Donnie Darko*.

I focused all my energy on Vyper, pretending she was the only one in the room. I could see out of the corner of my eye that the youths did, at least, look like they *understood* the tale of a scorned lover who wondered aloud if he could continue a sexual relationship with someone he argued with all the time. I think it's because I committed to the bit. They tell me I can't print the lyrics in this book, so go ahead and take a beat to hop on Spotify and listen to the Michael Bolton song if you're unfamiliar.

The Deaf Boys and Girls Club of Southeast Ohio witnessed something they likely did not expect when they arrived on campus that day. I'm certain those parents wouldn't let their kids step foot in a college classroom for years to come. As for myself, I pageant smiled through the remainder of the song with my head held high. I was proud I did such a good job, despite the awkwardness. The professor, however, was horrified by my performance. She gave me a C minus, telling me that she had to take off points for my misinterpretation of the assignment. I think she would've docked me more if she didn't know it was her own fault for not specifying that it had to be a kid-friendly song. I no longer remember how to sign the entire thing, but I can still do the chorus of "How Can We Be Lovers."

The experience taught me a valuable lesson about commitment. Sometimes we find ourselves in situations that are uncomfortable. Three minutes and fifty-five seconds in front of a crowd can feel like a lifetime, but you'll eventually get to the end of the song whether the children in the room like it or not. There are always going to be times that we want to run when life gets tough, and running is an option. You can head off to Tuscany and start a brand-new life under that Tuscan sun, or you can see something through with a smile on your face and, hopefully, a woman like Vyper in the audience. I think the most important thing I learned that day is to remember that life can always be worse. While I wish I would've signed a children's book and earned myself a higher letter grade, I'm so grateful that I didn't enter the classroom and sign about my pussy and my crack to the Deaf Boys and Girls Club of Southeast Ohio.

Epilogue

"Whats going on with mycareer"

CHER'S TWITTER (@CHER)

I opened this book talking about my adult journals and some of the ridiculousness found in the dried-up old pages. There was one entry from a particularly tough 2012 night that I thought I'd share as we wrap things up. It was years before my first entertainment gig. I hadn't made a penny off my writing, social media, or comedy, aside from a couple hundred dollars I earned doing a dinner theater show in Chicago. I felt like I was struggling to keep my head above water while everyone else seemingly had the career of their dreams (they didn't, but truth never gets in the way of feeling sorry for oneself). Here's a piece from that entry...

August 18

Dear Diary,

Someone told me that I look tired today but I'm not tired at all. It broke me—

Oops, that's the wrong day! Here's the actual entry I was referring to...

August 19

While my peers are finding success in areas they may not have initially been drawn toward, I'm stuck in limbo. When I left college, I didn't care that I was a struggling artist because my friends were also struggling to find jobs and make money. Now, those same people have risen in the ranks in their chosen professions. They have the money to go out to dinner when they want and buy clothes and nice things. I'm still wearing Old Navy hand-me-downs from a decade ago. They order steak and split checks evenly. I order a side salad with extra dinner rolls and have to pay my bill separately. They bring bottles of alcohol to share at house parties, and I'm like, "I didn't have a full bottle to bring, so I just got drunk before I came!" I'm embarrassed. I know that this is the price you pay for chasing dreams in your late twenties, but isn't that the point of all those movies we watched when we were eight? Why am I now the outcast for wanting something different in life? Friends and family are telling me to grow up, while they tell anyone under the age of twelve within spitting distance that they should "never give up on their dreams." I used to visualize those dreams coming true, but the older I get, the blurrier that vision becomes. I still hope I'll get there, but I feel like I'm going through life with protective eyewear on, and the more time that goes by, the dirtier they get. I'm losing sight of the life I want, but I'm not prepared to take off the glasses. Is seeing the world without the protection of my own hopes and dreams worse than fighting through the fog?

The entry reads like a low-budget Carrie Bradshaw, but I made it through that evening and I'm sharing in hopes that any of you who are feeling similarly might be able to fight through your own fog. I still don't have it all figured out, but I'm learning not to compare myself so much to other people. I'm not sure where I get off ending this as if it's some self-help guide instead of a collection of silly stories about Judy Garland and childhood trips to Florida, but when you put this book down, I implore you to do the same. Just because your best friend is sharing pictures of their perfect kids or your cousin is posting about a fancy job promotion, that doesn't mean they have it all together. Whether you're seventeen or seventy-four, just keep on doing you. We all have similar experiences to help us relate to each other, but we're on our own journeys. And although time may have a way of stealing our happiness, try to remember those childhood moments when everything seemed possible.

Recently I went to a Los Angeles restaurant with a pop-up Instagram installation. People crowded around to take pictures for social media, crafting the perfect captions and using the photo to show off to all their friends online. A few days later I flew to visit my family in Northeast Ohio, spending lots of time in early June with my nieces and nephews. As the sun set one night and an old Faith Hill song played on an outdoor speaker, I watched the kids running barefoot and happy on the green grass, and I thought about all the times I spent as a child catching fireflies in old mayonnaise jars at dusk in the same place. I gathered all the youngsters for an "Uncle Danny" photo, and although it was hard to get everyone to look at the camera, the lightning bugs lit our smiles more perfectly than the manufactured twinkle lights that are strewn together on a restaurant IG set ever could.

I often think about when I was their age, when my parents would assemble us in the unfinished basement before bed, and we would line up alongside the wall where there was a rickety piece of lumber barely attached to a doorway. My brothers and I would lean up against it one by one to mark our height. I would wear extra socks or stand on my tippy toes to gain a few extra centimeters. Dad would draw a line on the wood with a pen while Mom would tell him the date to write above the measurement. This repeated once a year, or whenever they would remember to corral us in the lower level. Our family of five gathered to mark time in between basketball practices, second jobs, mortgage payments, and puberty. That is, until we grew taller than the loose piece of timber. One by one we moved out of the house we grew up in and started our own families. My parents knew back then that life moves so quickly we must take a moment to acknowledge where we're at and look back at how far we've come. I tried my best to appear a little bit taller, to rush time, but now I'd give anything to go back and relive one of those nights exactly where I was, surrounded by the people I love most in a moment that was ours, when everything seemed possible. I hope that one day my nieces and nephews will hear that same Faith Hill song, think about those nights catching glowworms and feel the same, yearning to go back to a beautiful moment in time.

Nostalgia is a helluva drug, and although it's important to live in the now, I love knowing I have a bank of experiences I can escape to when the present is too much to handle. The reason I love '90s and early-aughts pop culture so much is because it helps me with my great escape, allowing me to time travel to those happy moments as often as I want. The things we look back on from our youth are more than just music, movies, TV shows, or toys; they are the quickest road to nostalgia, one of the easiest ways to recapture the feelings we had when we were our most innocent and optimistic selves, and the closest thing to getting into a time machine alongside Doc Brown.

My podcast usually ends by doing a little breathing exercise and sharing some cheesy motivational words. We get so caught up in our day-to-day that we forget to take a moment to catch our breath. So breathe in and breathe out. Measure your life not by the markings on the wood, but by the memories there within. Let the fireflies guide you through the fog, reminisce in the quiet of your mind, look back at how far you've come, and embrace the nostalgia. It's hard to *un-remember* the bad in life, but the good is a flashback away, and the sun will always rise to remind us that new memories start with the shine of the morning rays and continue through dusk.

Pictured left to right: Bryan, Dad, Jr., Mom, and me.

Acknowledgments

I know you thought you were done with this book, and you mostly are. However, I wanted to do a little acknowledgments section where I thank all the people who helped make this a reality, and I decided the acknowledgments section deserved a little detour of its own. This whole project wouldn't have been possible without my podcast audience, and my podcast wouldn't have happened without all the hours I've clocked watching talk shows.

Ever since I could remember, I've loved the talk interview format. As a little boy growing up in northeast Ohio, movies and television seemed less like a potential career path and more like a distant planet that I could never inhabit. Even so, I was enamored by the lifestyles of actors and musicians. Not only did it seem like they had all the money in the world, but they also got to create the things I loved most...movies! I watched stars talk about their latest work, and I dreamed of a different world, one filled with the magic of Hollywood that polished all of life's flaws and presented them in a pretty package. The guests were my way in, but I quickly fell more in love with the hosts of those shows.

When I was really young, my mom used to have Regis and Kathie Lee on in the morning, and I would marvel at their banter before school. Regis always knew how to find the punchline, unafraid to poke fun at himself in the process, while KLG had a unique ability to be silly one moment and serious the next without missing a beat, something she later honed even more with Hoda, who herself has such an obvious kindness in her soul that shines through the TV. Kelly Ripa would take over for Kathie Lee in 2001, and she had, and continues to have, such an effortlessly fun attitude. A lot of people praised Kelly's chemistry with Regis, but I think she could make chemistry with a cantaloupe if she had to. She's wildly charming. I've always just wanted to hang out with Kelly, and to this day, even though she has had tons of success, I'm not sure she is appreciated for just how phenomenal she is at her job.

Earlier I mentioned *The Rosie O'Donnell Show*, and there was a time when Rosie completely took over daytime. She was EVERYTHING to me. Every. Thing. Her love of pop culture and celebrity made me feel seen. Barbra Streisand, Mary Tyler Moore, Bette Midler, and more would guest, and Rosie would gush, unafraid to fangirl on air in front of millions of people. She was a pop culture junkie, just like us! When she would sit down at that desk and talk about the TV she watched the night before or the musical theater she took in, I felt like she was a bestie talking directly to me. She was a way for me to see Broadway shows without ever traveling to NYC, and the first influencer in my life. The Rosie O'Doll plush she released during the '90s along with the Rosie Barbie are both nestled safely in my office, but whatever she would promote, I would want, whether it be the toys and Koosh launchers she showcased on her desk, a book of "punny" jokes, a Tickle Me Elmo, or even her TWO holiday albums. That's right, Rosie made two Christmas albums, just like my other faves, Mariah Carey and Jessica Simpson. Icons only.

My mom liked Rosie, Regis, Kathie Lee, and Kelly, but Oprah was her number one. I've since gone back and watched old episodes of *The Oprah Winfrey Show*, stunned at how she could be so intelligent, while simultaneously being relatable and down to earth. The variety in those Oprah episodes is also something to be studied. One day we'd be watching her take a camping trip with Gayle, the next she would be talking to Julia Roberts, and later in the week there would be an hour on 9/11. Of course, we all also remember her Favorite Things episodes, which I still watch yearly, along with her Legend's Ball. One week when I had the flu recently, I watched the reality show she did for OWN about the making of the final season. It was so fascinating that I immediately started the series over to watch a second time right after I finished it. There will never be another Oprah.

Speaking of doing it all, I'd be remiss not to mention the greatest entertainer of all time who happened to also be a Popsicle stick, Stick Stickly. Stick was a Nickelodeon staple, and although not as respected as some of the other journalists here, I think about him all the time. It's a good reminder to all artists that you can be super creative with very few resources. You don't need a huge budget or A-list celeb guests to have a successful talk show. Googly eyes and a smile are enough.

In college, I became obsessed with *The View*, which I still watch every single day. Although it started long before my freshman year, Rosie's first tenure is what got me into it, and I believe the infamous split screen with Elisabeth Hasselbeck is one of the greatest hours of television of all time, regardless of genre. It was clearly difficult for the women to live through, but the tension is something scripted dramas could only dream of. "Go to commercial!" Joy shouted as I sat on the edge of my seat. Most people are familiar with the fight, but I also hop on YouTube from time to time to rewatch the segment that happened AFTER the split screen. Alicia Silverstone was there to talk about being a vegan, and she comes onstage moments after Rosie and Elisabeth had an intense back and forth about loyalty and the Iraq War. Alicia is visibly shook, out of breath, and unsure of herself. Ever the professionals, Joy, Sherri (who was filling in that day), Rosie, and Elisabeth all act as if it was all just a normal episode of television. It's FASCINATING.

I stuck with *The View* after Rosie left the first time, staying glued to the screen even during the Jenny McCarthy years. Some of the panels have been better than others, and it usually is reflected in the ratings, but I still love all the women who have sat at that table. With the rise of social media, I notice more and more people take to Twitter to voice their outrage at whoever is in the cast that they disagree with, but the truth is that show works best when there are a variety of voices for Hot Topics. I may not agree with the resident conservatives, but I recognize how important they are to make that hour succeed. There was a brief moment where they had a panel who mostly saw eye to eye and the Hot Topics leaned more toward pop culture than politics, which didn't make for a good show. Certain hosts deserved more (#Justice4MichelleCollins), others overstayed their welcome, but *The View* remains an institution, and I hope to still be watching a hologram of Whoopi, Joy, and the rest of the panel when I'm old and gray, getting fired up at whoever it is that I love to hate at the table.

For some reason men and women tend to be separated in the talk show space. Women largely occupy the daytime hours, while males fill up the late-night spots, which is unfortunate. Bonnie Hunt was a revelation in the afternoon for a couple of seasons, but I always thought she was too quick-witted for daytime, her jokes flying over the heads of people watching in the afternoon as they got dinner ready. I wish a network had given her a shot at a night spot when the audience is more concentrated on the material. I'd also love her to do more acting—quite frankly I just want more of her warm-hearted Midwest energy and humor wherever I can get it. These days I tune in to Andy Cohen before bed, his beautifully random mix of celebrity on *WWHL* is soothing to me. Where else on TV can you see Scheana from *Vanderpump Rules* alongside a CNN news anchor for an entire half hour?

There are a lot of great new hosts, people who offer their own blend of brilliance and fun. Kelly Clarkson is, to me, one of the greatest vocalists of our time, and I can't believe I live in a world where I can hear her perform a cover song every single day on her talk show! We also get Drew Barrymore's sunshine daily, and the ability of Wendy Williams to captivate an audience the way she does for twenty-some minutes at the top of every show BY HERSELF is inspiring.

The point is, I LOVE talk shows. I find myself in YouTube spirals at night watching old interviews, studying how Larry King would navigate his chats, seeing how Donny and Marie hosted as a duo, and being blown away by Katie Couric's ability to cover both hard news and fluff pieces.

When I decided to do my podcast, *Everything Iconic with Danny Pellegrino*, I didn't quite have the resources at my disposal to put on a huge show. As an independent production, I literally lost money the first two years, and in order to book guests, I had to plead with celebrities in their DMs. I wasn't backed by a network and had just a small social media following. I did, however, have all the lessons that I learned from my talk show heroes, and I truly believe that's what led to the show's success. Over the years, I have gotten the chance to chat with some of the hosts that I've admired from afar, something that I never could've imagined when I was that little boy in Ohio.

Rosie O'Donnell, Katie Couric, Andy Cohen, Kathie Lee Gifford, Marie Osmond, Bonnie Hunt...I've been fortunate enough to interview all of these talk show legends, and the one constant I've noticed in each of them is a warm spirit. They know how to make you feel like a friend, and I hope that when people listen to my show (or read this book), they think of me as one, and know that I think of you all as mine. Our worlds can be so lonely, but television, film, podcasts, and books are so important because they make us feel connected to the people around us, especially at times when we might be isolated.

Compared to these network juggernaut shows, my little podcast is inconsequential, but I feel incredibly proud of the work I've done. The fact I've had the opportunity to talk to some of these people means the world to me because it's my childhood dreams realized. One of the best sleeps of my life was the night after I interviewed Rosie, and that's because a goal that swirled in my head every night when I hit the pillow was finally checked off my list. There's a power that comes with making a dream a reality, and I'll continue to fantasize, but for now I want to say that I'm grateful for the lessons I've learned along the way, the talk show greats who have inspired me over the years, and most importantly, all of the people who listen, read, and follow.

Actual Acknowledgments

This book is a dream come true, and I'm FOREVER grateful to everyone who helped make it a reality. This little section might be gross to read, so I'm sorry in advance! Just tune it out if you're not interested. Also, why do I always feel the need to apologize for everything? Sorry for saying sorry so much. First and foremost, I want to thank the friends and family featured in the book. You're all so special to me, and I apologize if I got something wrong or upset any of you within the pages! It all comes from a place of love and admiration for all of you who have shared these stories with me.

My agent, Kristyn Keene Benton, is simply the best. Kristyn, you believed in this and me from the beginning. You're amazing, and I thank you for fighting for me and my vision for this book.

Kate Roddy, my editor at Sourcebooks, thanks for understanding me and this project! I loved working with you and everyone else at Sourcebooks, including Dominique Raccah, Liz Kelsch, Ashlyn Keil, the proofreaders, the graphics team, and everyone else who helped throughout the process. Kate, you were patient, kind, and helped elevate the book beyond my wildest expectations. You also made me look like a better writer, so I thank you for the beautiful editing work.

My ICM team, you're the best, and specifically thanks to Brittany Perlmuter for always listening to me vent.

Thank you to the Riker Brothers for taking the beautiful cover photo for me. I'm honored to call you both friends.

Mom and Dad, I love you both more than I can express in words. I hope you're not too mad about anything I wrote in here! You're the best parents a person could ask for. Mom, you have the biggest heart in the world, and I'm honored to be slowly morphing into you as I get older. You're my favorite person of all time. And Dad, you've taught me so many invaluable lessons about hard work and determination. This project wouldn't have come to fruition without the lessons you taught all of us about not giving up and always believing in yourself.

Bryan and Jr., I'm so glad I got to experience my childhood with the two of you by my side. I've always felt protected by your love and guidance. I'm lucky to have two big brothers who I know will always have my back.

Taryn and Samantha, I love you! I'm thrilled my brothers found such great women to join the family.

Anthony, Bella, Sophia, Brady, and Beckham, when you're old enough to read this, I hope you enjoy it and one day share your own Pellegrino memories. I love you, and I'm always here when you need me and when you don't.

Speaking of Pellegrinos, I've always had a deep connection with my grandma Rose, but it wasn't until I sat down to write this book that I realized just how important she was to me and continues to be.

She always found the good in people and led with kindness. Writing about my relationship with her provided closure that I didn't even know I needed, and I hope I go forward carrying a small part of her beautiful heart in mine. My grandma Sophie was also very important to me, the other side of the coin. I'll consider myself lucky to be even a tiny bit like her going forward. The two of them were the absolute best that life has to offer.

MP, you're my other favorite person in the world. I love you. I know I should say some specific things about you here, but there are too many things I like about you. I suppose I'm most grateful that I not only love you with all my heart, but that I like you so much too. Special thanks for all the amazing graphics you created for this project! And thanks to Mama P. (Shellie) for being so wonderful.

Babygirl/Jill, thanks for being my best friend and always believing in me, even in those moments I didn't always believe in myself. From our high school talent show to now, you've always been by my side cheering me on. Everyone needs a number one, and you're that for me. Xoxo.

Beth and Jude! You're always in my heart. I think back to all the times we would drive around together and talk about our hopes and dreams for the future. I'm grateful you both remained a part of my future and I'm happy to know you always will.

KTB! Thank you for letting me share a piece of our story. I love you SO MUCH. And you too, Tina D.! For always. We need another frienaissance soon!

Jenna B., I'm so grateful to have you in my creative circle. You're incredibly smart, kind, and creative, and I love being able to bounce things off you. Love you!

Hannah B., thanks so much for reading my work before it was work! I'm so grateful for our friendship.

Bob H., thank you for giving me a chance to be a writer when you hired me for your book. I learned so much about publishing. You opened a new world for me and took a chance on someone when you certainly didn't have to.

I've been fortunate enough to have some really great teachers in life, both in school and out. To all the people who taught me in a classroom and made me want to read and write, thank you. Teachers are WILDLY underappreciated, and I want to express appreciation from the bottom of my heart. From Mrs. Fabian in Kindergarten teaching me the basics of kindness, to Mrs. Kozel in middle school teaching me not to start sentences with the same word, Jill Frimel-Harvey for encouraging me to lead in high school, and Andrea Vecchio for being a great boss at a very impactful morning show internship at WKYC in Cleveland.

Andy Cohen, thank you for all the beautiful Bravo work you do, and for encouraging me to find a home for this book. I was ready to give up, and you gave me kind words when I needed them most.

Mariah Carey, I love you. "Forever" is my personal favorite song of yours because it has special meaning to me, but everything you've written and performed is iconic, and I need you to know how much I love you if by some insane chance you ever pick up this book. While we're here, I'd like to thank the entire cast and crew of VH1's *Divas Live 1998*.

Fozzie Bear, you're my first comedic influence and I will forever stan.

Nora Ephron, Meg Ryan, and Tom Hanks, thank you for creating my all-time favorite movie, *You've Got Mail*. It's the best and always lifts me up when I'm down. It's a perfect Christmas movie, but also works great as an autumnal viewing, or at the start of spring. Really, it's a year-round movie. I'll probs go watch it right now.

Finally, thank you all for reading this. I would send you each a bouquet of newly sharpened pencils if I had your addresses.

I'm overwhelmed with gratitude...but enough about me.

Xoxo

Danny

P.S. H.A.G.S. (Have a great summer!)

About the Author

Danny was raised in Solon, Ohio, and graduated from Kent State University. After graduation, he moved to Chicago, where he studied at The Second City and The iO Theater. He then made his way to Los Angeles, where he created the hit podcast *Everything Iconic with Danny Pellegrino*. The show frequently appears at the top of the podcast charts, with guests including Cameron Diaz, Katie Couric, Rosie O'Donnell, Keke Palmer, Elizabeth Olsen, Andy Cohen, Miss Piggy, and many more.

Danny took his podcast on the road with sold-out live shows across the country.

With a burgeoning screenwriting career, he has also co-authored two books, *Fancy AF Cocktails* and *The Super Carb Diet*.

He can be found on social media via @DannyPellegrino on Instagram and Twitter, or in front of the TV with a glass of bed wine.